TEXAS SKETCHES

TEXAS SKETCHES

A.C. GREENE

Illustrated by Paul Kolsti

TAYLOR PUBLISHING COMPANY
DALLAS, TEXAS

These sketches and drawings first appeared in
The Dallas Morning News. Rena Pederson originally suggested
their use as a newspaper feature. Most of the historical
pieces have been expanded and, in a few cases, the artwork has
been redrawn for publication in book form.

Library of Congress Cataloging-in-Publication Data

Greene, A.C., 1923-
    Texas sketches. Includes Index.

    1. Texas—History—Addresses, essays, lectures.
I. Title.
F386.5.G74   1985   976.4   85-17334
ISBN 0-87833-519-6

Printed in the United States of America

0 9 8 7 6 5 4 3 2 1

For all those new Texans who are helping to make history

Contents

TEXAS SKETCHES

The Founding of Austin

Austin alone among Texas cities was founded on beauty, the inspiration of Mirabeau Buonaparte Lamar, an impulsive poet who later became President of the Republic of Texas.

In 1837, when he was Vice President under Sam Houston, Lamar decided to take a vacation from both President Houston and the new capital city named for him. There was no love lost between Old Sam, the doer, and Lamar, the dreamer. Someone suggested that Lamar hunt buffalo up on the Colorado River above Bastrop, so the Vice President and his private secretary, the Reverend Edward Fontaine, set out for that Indian-haunted frontier. They got an escort of six rangers from Fort Colorado and rode west beside the Colorado to where Jacob Harrell had created a little stockade settlement he called Waterloo at the mouth of Shoal Creek. Harrell welcomed the hunters and early on the morning following their arrival, his young son woke everybody up shouting that the prairie was full of buffalo.

The Vice President and his party were soon in the saddle and the chase began. Lamar brought down the biggest bull any of the hunters had seen, dropping the buffalo in a valley where Congress Avenue and Seventh Street would someday cross in downtown Austin. Later the party was assembled by the bugler to the hill where the capitol now stands, and Lamar, stirred by the magnificent surroundings, exclaimed to Fontaine, "This should be the seat of Future Empire!"

Lamar was elected President in September of 1838 and one of his first official acts after assuming office was to appoint a commission, early in 1839, to locate a site for a new capital nearer the center of the Republic — nobody but Old Sam and the local merchants liked Houston. It is not surprising that when the commission reported back in April, Waterloo was the unanimous choice. The commission's account of the proposed site was poetic in its praise: "The imagination of even the romantic will not be disappointed on viewing the Valley of the Colorado and the fertile and gracefully undulating woodlands and luxuriant Prairies at a distance from it . . . and the citizen's bosom must swell with honest pride when, standing in the Portico of the Capitol, he looks abroad upon a region worthy only of being the home of the brave and the free."

The Republic paid $3 an acre for 7,700 acres of land to contain and surround the capital. The Texas Congress had taken care of political egos, stipulating that the new capital, wherever located, would be named for the late Stephen F. Austin, the father of Texas. Edwin Waller, who was later elected Austin's first mayor, began surveying the townsite and locating and erecting government buildings on May 21, 1839. On August 1 he conducted the town lot sale, disposing of 306 private parcels of land. The 640-acre townsite was laid out north of the Colorado River, between Shoal Creek on the west and Waller Creek, named for the surveyor, on the east. East-west streets were originally named for Texas trees (numeralized in the 1880s), while the north-south streets, save for Congress Avenue in the center and East and West avenues, were named for Texas rivers. Lamar and cabinet arrived October 17, 1839 to find an instant city awaiting their use.

City of Houston's Birth

Houston, like so many Texas cities, began as a real estate promotion. The founders were Augustus Chapman Allen and his younger brother, John Kirby Allen, natives of New York. They had come to Texas in 1832, moving to Nacogdoches where they became the pioneer real estate dealers of Texas and possibly its richest pair.

On August 25, 1836, the Allens paid Elizabeth Parrott, the widow of John Austin, the original grantee, $5,000 ($1,000 in cash and the rest in notes) for half a league of land (2,214 acres) along the west bank of Buffalo Bayou. Gail Borden (later the dairyman) and brother J.H., surveyed the townsite, and A.C. (as Augustus was called) supposedly used the top of his stovepipe hat to sketch the plat.

The Allens wasted no time promoting their town, which they named Houston in honor of Sam Houston, a friend of both. On August 30 they advertised in the Columbia (Tex.) newspaper that there was "no place in Texas more healthy," noting, "It is but a few hours sail down the bay (Galveston), where one may enjoy the luxuries of fish, foul (sic), oysters and sea bathing," and adding pointedly, "Nature appears to have designated this place for the future seat of government." John K., who a few days later was elected to the first Texas Congress, meeting in Columbia, declared he and his brother would build a two-story government building free if Houston were made capital of the Republic of Texas, and on November 30 it was so voted.

Francis R. Lubbock, who would later be governor and have a city named for him also, was aboard the *Laura,* first steamboat to reach Houston on January 1, 1837. It took the boat three days to push through Buffalo Bayou. Lubbock and a group took a yawl and went ahead to find Houston. The party missed the site, "there was so little evidence of a landing," said Lubbock. Going ashore, they found only "stakes and footprints . . . and a tent serving as a saloon."

The capital was moved to Houston in May 1837, with the statehouse at Main and Texas, later site of the Capitol Hotel, then the Rice Hotel. President Sam Houston was proud of "his"

city, noting on his April 26 arrival it had grown from a small log cabin and 12 persons to 100 finished houses and a population of 1,500. A huge boost in population occurred in January of 1837 when the rest of the Allens — mother, father, a sister and four more brothers — reached Houston.

The founders were not so fortunate as their city. John K., despite the advertised healthy climate, contracted malaria and died unmarried and without a will in 1838 at age 28, and is buried in Founders Park. By 1843 the parents were dead and A.C. became embroiled with his brothers over John's inheritance and in 1850 his wife Charlotte, who had bankrolled many of the Allens' early enterprises, became dissatisfied with the settlement of the business and they separated. Augustus moved to Mexico, broken in health, and never came back to Houston. He died in Washington, D.C. in 1864 and was buried in Brooklyn.

Texas' First Motorbus

The first intercity motorbus line in Texas ran between Colorado City and Snyder in West Texas. The first scheduled trip was made Monday, October 29, 1907. The vehicle was one of the very first commercially designed intercity buses in the United States. Called a stagecoach, it carried 14 passengers and had solid tires with a chain drive. W.B. Chenoweth, the bus line promoter, leased the Borbein Automobile Co. shops in St. Louis to build two bodies to his design. Borbein did not make motors so Chenoweth had Western Motor Co. of Logansport, Indiana build two six-cylinder motors at a cost of $735 each. The first vehicle was completed in four months, with virtually every part handmade. It was tested in St. Louis then shipped to Colorado City on a railroad flatcar. (Chenoweth began his line in Colorado City because a banker there who was a motor enthusiast had had Chenoweth drive a new Lambert automobile for him from Fort Worth.)

Leonard G. Simon, who became an executive with railroad, air and bus lines, recalled as a boy being allowed to ride on the rear step of the Chenoweth bus as it chugged around Colorado City, his hometown. Simon, writing of the affair in later years, said the bus had no muffler and was so noisy the West Texans thought it would explode. One preacher warned his congregation to keep a safe distance.

On the maiden trip, with Chenoweth and W.A. (Uncle Bill) Jones, a Snyder investor, aboard, people were warned beforehand to keep off the road with horses. But en route, two cowboys on horseback forced the bus to stop and remain motionless until they got by. There was no road between the two towns and the bus was stuck in a ditch for hours, arriving in Snyder at 9 P.M. The whole town came down to the square to see the first self-propelled vehicle in that part of the country. On the return trip, five passengers rode only when offered free rides. Thereafter business was fairly good until citizens "invited" Chenoweth to take his noisy contraption elsewhere. He moved to Big Spring and the second vehicle arrived, to join the first in making the 55 miles to Lamesa in eight or nine hours.

Again, Chenoweth was modestly successful, but a local cattleman bought four Model F two-cylinder Buicks to compete. Chenoweth began operating 30 miles from Snyder to Roscoe, but a few weeks later a hardware store owner bought two five-passenger two-cylinder Reo touring cars as new competition, and Chenoweth left the field, taking his buses to Fort Worth where they were converted to trucks and sold to a dairy. One engine was quickly ruined by being driven without oil or water and was dragged home by a team of horses. Chenoweth, living near Dallas, died in 1954.

The Survivors of The Alamo

Even the most loyal Texan knows that some of the "facts" we supposedly know about the Battle of the Alamo are questioned: Did Col. W.B. Travis draw a line with his sword and invite all who wished to stay to step over? Did Davy Crockett surrender, and was he then shot? How many survivors were there in the Alamo itself?

None of these is more uncertain than the latter. Some Texans will respond, "There were no survivors," but most will remember Suzanna Dickenson and her baby, Angelina, "The Babe of the Alamo," and Travis' slave Joe, or recall the story of Louis Rose, who refused to step over the line — if there was a line. However, these were but a few of the list of known or possible survivors. Amelia Williams, in an authoritative series in the 1934 *Southwestern Historical Quarterly,* wrote, "All agree, no white male inmate (defender) of the Alamo remained alive," but says 15 or more persons were spared, including Bowie's slave, Sam; Mrs. Horace Alsbury, her 18-month-old son Alijo Perez, and her 15-year-old sister Gertrudis Navarro; Mrs. Gregorio Esparza, 8-year-old Enrique and three younger sons; Mrs. Toribio Losoya and three young children; Trinidad Saucedo, supposed to have been a beautiful young girl; Dona Petra, a very old woman; possibly Anselmo Borgarra, a noncombatant and first to reach Gonzales with news of the March 6 disaster; and Madam Candalaria, of whom there is question, although the Texas Legislature gave her a pension.

Mexican accounts say there were eight to 10 other Mexican women and a number of small children present, but there is probably some overlap here. In 1968, Walter Lord, writing in *The Republic of Texas,* describes some defenders he thinks may have escaped: Brigido Guerrero, who said he missed death by telling the Mexican soldiers he had been a prisoner of the Texans; Henry Warnell, an ex-jockey from Arkansas who, though wounded, escaped to Port Lavaca only to die of his wounds a few months later (Amelia Williams says he was sent as a messenger before the final battle); and two mysterious men, one badly wounded, who appeared in Nacogdoches in mid-March of 1836

a week before the official Alamo news arrived, claiming they had escaped and telling of the garrison being put to the sword. Their story appeared in the *Arkansas Gazette* but no names were given. Walter Lord also believes the last messenger from the Alamo was 16-year-old James L. Allen, not John W. Smith, as is generally held. Allen rode to Goliad but survived to become later mayor of Indianola.

Cisco's Santa Claus Bank Robbery

On December 23, 1927, Santa Claus and three helpers set out to rob a bank. It happened in Cisco, Texas and became the most bizarre bank robbery in American history. The four men held up the First National Bank, the leader wearing the Santa mask and suit because Cisco had been his home and he was well known there. He thought in the Christmas season a Santa Claus outfit would be a perfect disguise.

From the beginning the episode was a comedy of errors — and death. A little girl saw "Santa Claus" enter the bank and she dragged her mother along so she could tell Santa one last wish. When she and her mother entered the front door of the bank and saw men with drawn guns, the girl started crying, "They're going to kill Santa Claus!" and because the hold-up men weren't hard-hearted enough to harm them, the mother and the girl ran through the bank and out a rear door, screaming the alarm. Spurred by a well publicized $5,000 "Dead Bank Robber" reward, offered by Texas bankers, within minutes the bank was surrounded by armed citizens, some of whom had gone into hardware stores and grabbed up guns from stock.

The robbers shot their way through the ambush to their getaway car, stolen the night before, only to discover within a couple of miles that the gasoline gauge was showing empty. They had forgotten to fill the tank after driving the stolen vehicle from Wichita Falls. Then, when they held up another car in order to take it, the 14-year-old driver calmly pocketed the ignition keys and walked away and hid. An armed posse was right on their tails, so the robbers jumped back in the first car and fled again — in their rush leaving behind a dying companion and everything they had taken in the robbery.

By that time not only was one of them dying, two Cisco policemen, including the chief, were dead. The manhunt that ensued was the biggest in Texas history, involving several sheriffs, dozens of citizens, and the Texas Rangers under the famous Captain Tom (Ace) Hickman. This was the first time the Rangers used an airplane in a search, sending Ranger M.T. (Lone Wolf) Gonzaullas aloft in an open cockpit plane to scour a section of

13

Brazos River bottoms near Graham. It took a week for the three remaining hold-up men to be caught. Ultimately, one of the robbers was given life, one was electrocuted, and on November 19, 1929, after he had mortally wounded a jailer, a mob broke into the Eastland County jail, pulled out "Santa Claus" and lynched him by hanging, so that eventually, six men died from Cisco's grim Christmas crime caper.

First Railroad in Texas

One of the initial acts of the first Congress of the Republic of Texas in 1836 was to charter the Texas Railroad, Navigation and Banking Co., and although the project was supported by some of the most illustrious names in Texas history, it was successfully opposed by Anson Jones because of its banking provisions. But ambitious rail schemes continued to be chartered in Texas, mostly involving the Brazos River, Buffalo Bayou, and Galveston, the major port of that day. As early as July 1840, grading was done and ties bought by Andrew Briscoe for the Harrisburg Railroad and Trading Co., which was planned as a transcontinental line starting from Harrisburg on Buffalo Bayou.

In 1847 Gen. Sidney Sherman (originator of "Remember the Alamo!") took over the stalled project and collected Boston capital for the venture, obtaining a state charter in February, 1848, for the Buffalo Bayou, Brazos and Colorado Railroad. Not until late in 1852 was actual work begun. Harrisburg, long since a part of Houston, was the eastern terminus and Richmond 30 miles west was to be the crossing point on the Brazos. The gauge was 4 feet 8½ inches, which became standard for U.S. railroads. Much of the construction cost was to come from the sale of lots in Harrisburg. The road was planned deliberately to miss Houston, considered a competitor. The first locomotive, the "General Sherman," arrived at Galveston in December 1852 — the second locomotive west of the Mississippi.

It was not until August of 1853 that 20 miles of rail had been laid to Stafford's Point (now Stafford), which insured survival under the railroad's charter. Officially, service began September 9. A Galveston *News* advertisement stated that on Wednesday and Saturday at 9 A.M. cars with passengers and freight would leave Harrisburg for Stafford's Point, returning at 12 noon. There were no Sunday trains. Passengers were carried in four-wheel carriages which one observer said had originally been Boston streetcars. The BBB&C finally reached the Brazos opposite Richmond in 1855, then made it to the San Barnard River in 1859 and Eagle Lake later that year, and in the fall of

1860 reached Alleyton on the east bank of the Colorado where it stopped until after the Civil War. In 1870 the road's name was changed to Galveston, Harrisburg and San Antonio Railroad, and in 1877 it became the first railroad to reach San Antonio. The timetable for that year showed one train daily from San Antonio to Houston, but, alas, no passenger service at all to Harrisburg. In 1888 the Harrisburg shops were rebuilt in Houston, future headquarters for all the Southern Pacific roads in Texas. Southern Pacific later absorbed the GH&SA. Thus, the first railroad in Texas remains in operation under the SP name.

San Antonio Irrigation

Perhaps the most important contribution the San Antonio missions made to Texas has been overlooked: the intricate and successful irrigation system installed by the Spanish. Not only did the *acequias* or "ditches" help build the city, their long use was instrumental in the formation of some of Texas' present day water laws.

The oldest of the San Antonio canals was the Concepcion, constructed in 1729. Its dam was near the old Mill Bridge over the San Antonio River. The canal ran along Mission Road and Roosevelt Street, thence to the mission and its lands. Edwin P. Arneson, in a 1921 *Southwestern Historical Quarterly*, wrote that this *acequia* was large enough for the fathers to use a boat on its waters to and from the mission. The canal was abandoned in 1869.

The San Pedro *acequia* was started in 1738 to furnish water for the village of San Fernando de Bexar and was six feet wide, two feet deep and four miles long. Its headgate was at San Pedro springs and its course later became North Flores street along Main Plaza and then down a ridge between the San Antonio River and San Pedro creek. This *acequia* provided water for the fifteen Canary Islander families, the 1731 pioneers who set up the first civil government in Texas.

The Alamo *madre* was dug between 1718 and 1744, taking water from the San Antonio River above Brackenridge Park and eventually going six miles to irrigate 900 acres of Alamo mission land. The San Jose mission canal was built about 1730, using the waters of San Pedro creek near its mouth. It continued in use until 1860. The Upper Labor canal was started in 1776 as a civilian undertaking. Its headworks were also at the head of the San Antonio River and from there ran around Tobin Hill to empty into San Pedro Creek.

Two of the *acequias* are still in partial use. The San Juan canal, dug in 1731, began on the east side of the river opposite the San Jose ruins, and still carries water. The last *acequia* on the river is the one which furnished water for the Espada mission and continues to operate today. This is probably the most visited

ditch because of its two-arch stone aqueduct across an arroyo. It has survived over 250 years of often heavy floods. Legend says the structure's excellence was guaranteed by mixing the whites of thousands of eggs and much goat's milk in the mortar. Water wheels, lifting water from the *acequias* to the individual plots, were long a picturesque feature of San Antonio. Irrigation land units were given numbers and a drawing was offered applicants in mission days. In this way a plot became known as a *suerte,* from the Spanish word for luck. Arneson called the Spanish irrigation ditches "the earliest furrows of civilization in Texas."

The Galveston Flood

From the days of the Republic of Texas, Galveston was the richest, the most elegant and most sophisticated of all Texas cities, and for several decades it was also the largest city in the state. Its port ranked very high in national importance and most of the foreign newcomers to the Southwest, particularly immigrants from Europe, entered by way of Galveston. As early as 1845 the city established the first chamber of commerce in Texas, and through the 19th century its famous residents extended from William Rice, whose legacy created Rice University, and Gail Borden, founder of the dairy empire, to Jack Johnson, the great black world champion heavyweight boxer, and Albert Lasker, genius of the modern advertising business.

Then, on the afternoon of September 8, 1900, the great hurricane, or Galveston Flood, as it was called, struck. The entire island, which was only nine feet above sea surface at its highest point, was submerged. Winds as high as 120 mph blew a tidal wave across the island, putting the city under from four to seven feet of water for several hours. Half of Galveston's structures were destroyed, and not a single one escaped damage. An estimated $30-40 million worth of property was destroyed, millions more simply disappeared. At least 6,000 residents (probably many more) died in the greatest natural disaster in United States history. As soon as possible, women and children were evacuated to the mainland but the men were forced to remain, not only to clean up but to search for the dead. Attempts to dump the dead at sea resulted in thousands of corpses washing back onto the shore. Eventually a mass cremation was performed on the thousands of bodies never identified.

But many improvements came out of the tragedy. From 1902 to 1904 Galveston County built a massive 17-foot concrete seawall facing the Gulf of Mexico (the wall now extends 10 miles), then, once the seawall was completed, the city's grade was raised as much as 15 feet behind the seawall, which required jacking up and filling under some 2,000 buildings, raising water and sewer pipes and streetcar tracks, as well as the streets themselves, and whatever trees and shrubbery homeowners wished to salvage.

This task, unequaled in municipal history, was completed in 1910.

Within a year after the hurricane, Galveston had introduced a semi-appointive form of commission city government to the world, basing the need for strong municipal control on the tremendous management job to be done if the city were to survive. Court cases forced all five commissioners to be elected, and before long Galveston was being called "the best governed city on the American continent." The commission form of government eventually led to the city manager system.

The seawall has proved effective in the years since its erection. For example, an August 1915 hurricane with winds of 120 mph flooded the business section with five to six feet of water and cost 275 lives and $50 million in damage — but the seawall prevented a repetition, or worse, of the 1900 disaster.

El Paso Del Norte

In 1981 El Paso celebrated its four hundredth anniversary, not as a city but a place, the famed *"el paso del norte,"* or "The Pass of the North," along the Rio Grande, giving it the longest continuous history of any part of Texas. Even though the east (Texas) side of the river was not settled until after 1827, the "pass" itself was on what is now the Texas side.

Members of the Rodriquez-Chamuscade expedition of 1581 were the first Europeans to cross the river (at Frontera, now within the Texas city) and use the pass. Juan de Oñate, on his way to found New Mexico in 1598, made it the colonial gateway. A settlement called El Paso, or Paso del Norte, grew up on the west (Mexican) side of the river and in 1668 the church still standing (in Juarez) was dedicated.

The Pueblo Revolt of 1680, which drove the Spanish out of northern New Mexico, sent 2,000 refugees to the El Paso area and saw the establishment of the small El Paso valley towns of Ysleta, Socorro and San Elizario (a change in the river's course in 1849 put all three in Texas). Don Diego de Vargas in 1691 led the Spanish from El Paso on the (somewhat) peaceful reconquest of New Mexico. The first American to leave a record of the area, Lt. Zebulon Pike, while a Spanish prisoner in 1807, wrote of El Paso, "The settlement is by far the most flourishing (Spanish) town we have been in . . . finely cultivated fields of wheat and numerous vineyards from which were produced the finest wine ever drank." In 1888 the Mexican city of El Paso del Norte was renamed Ciudad Juarez, to honor the Mexican president who made it capital-in-exile in 1865-66.

The Texas city has been known by different names, although as historian C.L. Sonnichsen points out, the post office (since 1852) has always been El Paso. In 1827 Juan Maria Ponce de Leon established El Rancho de Ponce where downtown El Paso, Texas stands, the first settlement on the east bank. In 1846, the United States Army captured Paso del Norte after a brief battle near today's Sunland Park (N.M.), and the river became an international boundary. Ben Franklin Coons bought the de Leon land in 1849, setting up a town of sorts, and in 1858 when the

Butterfield Overland Mail Co. had Anson Mills build its largest and most important station there (covering two acres between El Paso and Oregon streets), the town was still being called Franklin City. But Magoffinsville was nearby (where Fort Bliss was first established in 1854), and below it was Concordia, while the name Smithville was sometimes used after William T. (Uncle Billy) Smith bought out Coons.

The wandering of downtown El Paso streets can be credited to Uncle Billy's generosity. He gave away many plots of land to friends, letting them erect homes as they would, and when Mills, the district surveyor, began laying out a townsite in 1858, the founding fathers would not let him move anybody to accomplish the usual gridiron street pattern. It was Mills who gave the resulting town the name of El Paso.

During the Civil War the El Paso region was the only part of Texas captured and held by the Union. Volunteer Union troops called the California Column chased out the Confederates in August 1862, and after the war several of these Unionists remained to run El Paso for a decade or more.

The Telegraph and Texas Register

The earliest Texas newspaper to achieve what historian E.W. Winkler called "a degree of permanence" was *The Telegraph and Texas Register.* Begun in 1835 at San Felipe de Austin (the seat of Stephen F. Austin's colony) by Gail Borden, Jr., Thomas H. Borden and Joseph Baker, the paper became the official voice of the Republic of Texas when formed in 1836. The approach of Santa Anna's army caused the publishers to flee San Felipe for Harrisburg on Buffalo Bayou after issuing the March 24, 1836 edition. The April 14 issue was being "put to bed" at Harrisburg (now part of Houston) when Santa Anna's army again interrupted, capturing the printers and tossing the press into the bayou.

In the summer of 1836, Gail Borden obtained a new press in Cincinnati and resumed publication at Columbia where the Texas Congress was sitting. The August 30 issue carried the first advertisement for the new city of Houston. In April 1837, the press was loaded aboard the steamer *Yellow Stone* and taken to Houston, now designated capital of the Republic. Renamed the *Houston Telegraph,* the first issue there was May 2, 1837. The Bordens soon sold out to Francis Moore, Jr., and Jacob Cruger.

After an up-and-down period, part of the time under ownership of H.H. Allen, a younger brother of Houston's founders, a stock company was formed in 1856 and offered the editorship to Edward H. Cushing, a young Vermonter who had come to Texas directly out of Dartmouth College to teach. Cushing eventually became sole owner and during the Civil War, when Federal forces closed the Mississippi River, he organized a pony express to gather and forward war news. In that period the *Telegraph* was sometimes printed on butcher's paper or wallpaper.

Cushing spent the summer of 1865 "up North" acquiring new mechanical equipment and taking the pulse of the late enemy. On returning to Houston, he wrote stirring editorials counseling acceptance of Federal rule and saying such things as, "Let us now do all we can for (ex-slaves) as free black people, morally, intellectually, and legislatively." (In spite of this attitude,

Reconstruction Governor E.J. Davis wrote a letter to President Andrew Johnson protesting the granting of a political pardon to Cushing, suggesting he be hanged instead.) But a conciliatory editor was resented, and Cushing was forced to sell the news operation, retaining the job printing department and becoming publisher of several books by Texas authors, among them the poems of Mollie E. Moore, Maud Young's *Botany of Texas* and John Sayles' *Practice.*

But without Cushing the *Telegraph* lost ground and after a succession of widely different leaderships, suspended publication in the fall of 1873. It was revived in March 1874 by A.C. Gray who made it into a daily, and for a time it had the largest circulation ever obtained by a Houston newspaper, but creditors eventually forced suspension, and on February 11, 1877, the *Telegraph* ceased to exist.

John Neely Bryan: Father of Dallas

The "father" of Dallas was John Neely Bryan, a 31-year-old bachelor from Tennessee. Although he first visited Texas in 1835, Bryan didn't get to "The Three Forks", as the upper Trinity River region was called, until about 1840, when he rode what is now Preston Road to look over the country. He found what he was looking for: an 18-foot bluff, where he felt he could develop a town. It was the head of navigation of the Trinity and a well-known crossing of the river. He is said to have burned his name on pieces of hide and staked out a claim before going back to the Red River settlements, but this seems to be legend, and was not the method used in "staking claims" in Texas.

Bryan returned to The Three Forks in October 1841 to help build Bird's Fort in present day Tarrant County. Then, around November 9, 1841, with four other bachelors, he attempted to start his town. One of his companions remembered the first structure they lived in as "an open face hunters lean-to."

Neely Bryan rode a horse with the Choctaw Indian name of *Neshoba,* which meant gray wolf, and he was accompanied by a bear-dog he called Tubby. The dog wasn't fat. It was named for a Choctaw chief, either Moshulatubbee or Higholetubbee ("-tubbee" was a Choctaw war name, signifying "killer"). Bryan confused historians by naming several mounts "Neshoba," thus appearing to ride the same horse for decades.

Bryan's bluff is now Dealey Plaza in downtown Dallas. In 1841 the river ran about where the Triple Underpass is today. He lived in a dugout, but when he married Margaret Beeman in February of 1843, he had a log cabin built for her, there on the bluff. However, this was not the so-called "Bryan Cabin" on display at Memorial Plaza.

Bryan had clerked at Holland Coffee's station on the Red River, and had lived and traded with the Cherokee and Choctaw Indians, reputedly speaking seven dialects. He was said to be a lawyer but no record of his license has been found. He was also said to have helped develop Van Buren, Arkansas, but this is not verified. Bryan was apparently well educated and brought several books with him to his frontier home.

Dallas' First Law Suits

One thing early settlers of Dallas complained about most was the distance they had to travel to do simple legal business, such as transfer of deeds and obtaining a marriage license. That part of Dallas which today lies west and southwest of the Trinity River was in Robertson County, with Old Franklin, the county seat, 150 miles south, while the portion east and north of the river was in Nacogdoches County, whose seat was the same distance east.

When Dallas County was created in the spring of 1846 and Dallas was designated temporary county seat, local inhabitants were delighted — and one civil case resulted in a pretty romance. The first Dallas County Grand Jury brought in 61 indictments, including 51 (against males) for gaming. Since this took in just about every man in town (and only males served on juries) the first ones convicted had to step over and serve as jury for the others in turn. Each of the 51 drew a $10 fine — quite steep for a day and time when cash was scarce and $10 was not a bad monthly salary. It would be interesting to have more details as to what sort of gaming it was.

The first civil suit in Dallas County was heard in December 1846, when Charlotte M. Dalton, daughter of John Huitt, the county's first sheriff, sued husband Joseph Dalton for divorce. The jury granted the divorce, and a few hours later the former Mrs. Dalton married Henderson Couch, foreman of the jury. History doesn't give us much on Joseph Dalton, unless he was the Dalton listed as a Peters Colonist in 1853. Couch was a 35-year-old widower with two children when he married Charlotte. As her father had settled at Cedar Springs in 1843, the same year Couch received a land grant nearby, there is a good chance Henderson and Charlotte had known each other prior to the divorce. At any rate, following their marriage they went to live on his farm, which today would include much of Highland Park, west of Preston Road, between Beverly Drive and Hawthorne.

Cedar Springs in Dallas

Cedar Springs, as a place and a name, is older than Dallas. An Indian village had been on the site prior to 1840. In February 1841, when soldiers of the Republic of Texas erected a temporary post at Cedar Springs, the location was already well known. Dallas began (if four or five bachelor hunters make a beginning) nine months later. The post at the springs was the first structure erected by white men in Dallas County. Apparently it was never garrisoned, but was used by troops laying out the Military Road, which stretched from Holland Coffee's Station on the Red River, via Cedar Springs and the Kickapoo Crossing of the Trinity (in downtown Dallas), to Austin.

When Dr. John Cole and his five sons arrived at Cedar Springs in the fall of 1843, Dr. Cole planned to claim the springs as part of his Peters Colony grant. But he discovered the area had already been granted to Crawford Grigsby, a Texas Revolution veteran. Cole had to pay $160 (about one dollar an acre) to the Grigsby heirs to obtain ownership of the springs.

The doctor put up a log mercantile establishment and drug store, and a town with church, school, and race track began to grow along the creek formed by the springs. After Cole's death in 1850, Cedar Springs Institute opened. Gold and Donaldson built a distillery in conjunction with their grist mill at the springs, producing a reputable grade of whiskey selling for 50¢ a gallon. William A. Gold died and Donaldson sold out to a Mr. Wheeler, referred to as "a northern man." Wheeler ran the mill and distillery successfully for about two years, then both burned. Wheeler attempted to rebuild but before he could complete the work, he was thrown from a horse and killed. Cedar Springs whiskey remained a Dallas staple until after the Civil War, however.

In 1850 Dallas beat out Hord's Ridge and Cedar Springs in the county seat election, although citizens cried foul: Dallas, they claimed, had gotten the Cedar Springs voters drunk. Today, Cedar Springs Road remains a major Dallas street, and some of the springs still flow, although now submerged in the creek. The townsite was mainly situated around the modern crossing of Cedar Springs and Kings Road.

The Military Post of Fort Worth

Construction of a United States Army post on the West Fork of the Trinity was begun in May 1849, by Maj. Ripley Arnold, with Middleton Tate Johnson, of Johnson's Station (now Arlington) as guide. It was the northernmost in a line of forts beginning west of San Antonio, and continuing by Austin, the Waco Village, and Dallas.

Maj. Arnold's company of 42 dragoons first camped below Cold Springs near the Trinity River, but a July flood sent the troops scrambling up a bluff to higher ground, and after dispossessing civilian Press Farmer and family, who were living in a tent on the proposed military site, the soldiers began building Camp Worth, named for General William Jenkins Worth, commander of U.S. forces in Texas, who died about the time construction began. Camp Worth was designated Fort Worth in mid-November.

The post consisted of 20 buildings, including stables. All were of logs and, according to an inspector's report, were leaky and unsubstantial. Lt. W.H.C. Whiting, an engineer, complained (officially) that the stables were "much too near the quarters . . . and cannot but be offensive in summer." Maj. Arnold was a dashing aristocrat who brought his wife Catherine and their five children to the post the summer of 1850, and it is said her piano accompanied her. But the summer was a sad one for the Arnolds as two of their children died. Arnold, who spoke excellent French, employed Adolphe Gouhenant (often referred to as "Dr. Gounah"), of New Icaria, the ill-fated utopian experiment in Denton County, to teach his officers swordsmanship and social dancing. The military post saw little service, and because the Indians had moved farther west, Fort Worth was abandoned in September 1853. At that same time, Maj. Arnold, on duty at Fort Gates, was murdered by a fellow officer.

Fort Worth was located on land which today lies immediately west of the Tarrant County courthouse, between Bluff and Weatherford, Houston and Throckmorton streets.

The Name of Dallas

Dallas *County* was named in 1846 for Vice President George Mifflin Dallas. But who was the *City* of Dallas named for? For nearly a century, the question plagued historians, several names being suggested. We now have a historically sound idea.

George Mifflin Dallas was a Philadelphia lawyer, hardly known outside his home state until he was put on the presidential ticket with James K. Polk in mid-1844. He and Polk successfully campaigned for the annexation of Texas to the U.S., and that's why Dallas County honors him. But the town was called "Dallas" well before George Mifflin Dallas gained prominence. A deed filed in August of 1842 is for a lot in "Bryan's town of Dallas," and the name had obviously been chosen earlier. It is highly unlikely that John Neely Bryan, the founder of Dallas, would have known the Philadelphia lawyer, but his older brother, U.S. Navy Commodore Alexander James Dallas, is another matter.

New historical evidence suggests Bryan staged a contest, offering a town lot to whoever supplied a name for his proposed town. The contest was won by Charity Gilbert, the first white female to live in Dallas and wife of Captain Mabel Gilbert. Since Bryan proposed his new town should be a river port, she suggested "Dallas" to honor Commodore Dallas, commander of the U.S. Navy's Gulf of Mexico squadron. (The deed to the lot Bryan gave her has been found.)

Mrs. Gilbert was a member of the Morris family of Pennsylvania, friends of the Dallas family. Commodore Dallas, a national hero who fired the first return shot in the War of 1812, had been stationed at New Orleans and was a friend of her husband and his brother, both riverboat captains. Bryan chose the site primarily because it was the head of navigation for the Trinity River; his interest in having Gilbert, the riverboat captain move to his "town" was not at random. Coincidentally, Charity and Mabel had with them a parrot, Jocko, when they arrived at Bryan's bluff on March 1, 1842. And where do you think the parrot came from? It was a gift from Commodore Dallas.

Preston Road: Older Than Dallas

There's a well-known street in Dallas that's older than the city itself, and named after a 19th century Gomorrah. It was already a famous trail when John Neely Bryan used it, locating his town of Dallas. The trail was favored by travelers because it followed the watershed ridge between the East Fork and the Elm Fork of the Trinity and there were no large streams to cross.

That trail is now Preston Road. It began in Grayson County at Holland Coffee's trading house on the Red River (now beneath the waters of Lake Texoma) and led south almost 100 miles to the ford on the Trinity (now downtown Dallas) where Bryan stopped. In 1840 the Republic of Texas sent Col. William Cooke to lay out the Military Road and establish certain outposts from Austin to Coffee's Station, and the upper portion of this road followed the trail.

Preston family tradition has it that a warehouse at Coffee's Station was dubbed "Fort" Preston, for William Gilwater Preston, a young officer said to have been in charge of service and supply. But the name is not found in records of the Cooke expedition. In 1845 Coffee had a town named Preston surveyed at his station, and soon even the bend in the Red River was called Preston Bend. The town was notorious for its debauchery and lawlessness. Coffee — no saint, himself — was killed in a knife fight on its streets in 1846. The southward trail leading to and from the town became "the Preston road." Warren Angus Ferris, surveying the north line of Dallas County in 1850, referred to it as "the Coffee Bend Road."

Thousands of settlers poured down Preston Road, and thousands of cattle went up it in the days before railroads. Today the Dallas thoroughfare follows Bryan's path rather closely; and one may take Highway 289 north from Dallas and, after some twists in the road, come to where Preston Road literally disappears beneath Lake Texoma's waters.

New Icaria

In the early spring of 1848 a group of French followers of Etienne Cabet arrived in southern Denton County to set up a utopian colony called New Icaria. The name, and the inspiration, came from Cabet's communistic novel, *Voyage to Icaria.* Cabet urged the colonizing scheme in 1847 with his proclamation, *Allons en Icarie.*

From the Peters Colony the Icarians obtained land at the confluence of Oliver and Denton creeks, about one mile northeast of the present town of Justin. The first group built one log house and some sheds, surveyed about 100 square miles of land, and planted some wheat — but few such utopian groups were as poorly equipped to survive the Texas wilderness as these political philosophers. Of the first 69 arrivals, a dozen died before 1848 was out: four from fever, seven from fatigue (probably sun and heatstroke), and one from being struck by lightning. Five others defected during July. Only a few newcomers joined the survivors, although a second party of from 500 to 1,500 families was promised by Cabet, who was a great dreamer. A second group of New Icarians left France in June 1848, but only ten arrived at the Denton County site. These decided to leave, but six died fleeing to New Orleans.

Leadership of the colony was assumed by Adolphe Gouhenant who is referred to by some historians as a medical doctor but who actually was an artist with no medical training. New Icaria lasted only about a year. Cabet sailed from France for New Orleans with 450 prospective colonists in January 1849, but 200 of them withdrew from his leadership and he and the rest decided to remain in New Orleans. By that time the Texas project was a disaster, and Cabet's followers bought the old Mormon settlement at Nauvoo, Illinois, renaming it "Icaria." Cabet presided until 1855, enduring squabbles and lawsuits, becoming an American citizen in 1854.

A handful of Icarians, including Gouhenant, remained in the Dallas-Fort Worth area and became respected citizens. In 1886 the Santa Fe Railway is said to have made a gravel pit of the Icarian farmlands.

The Bryans' Wedding

John Neely Bryan, founder of Dallas, knew what he was doing in the winter of 1842 when he journeyed from his proposed "town" west to Bird's Fort and persuaded the John Beeman family to join him. This 32-year-old bachelor lived in a dugout where Dealey Plaza in downtown Dallas is today. To put it plainly, he was lonesome — and he knew John Beeman had two pretty daughters, because he had met the family earlier in another part of Texas. (One wonders if Bryan also wanted a wife to assure himself of a full 640-acre land grant; bachelors got only half that number of acres.)

Although the Beeman family located on White Rock Creek, several miles east of Neely Bryan (about the 3400 block of Forney Road), it didn't take him long to start wooing 17-year-old Margaret, the youngest daughter, and win her hand. But to get married legally they had to travel north to try and find a justice of the peace or some other qualified official — and that meant four or five days on the road together. Legend says Bryan signed a pledge vowing her "safety."

Bryan family records (written after the event) show Neely and Margaret to have married February 26, 1843 at Pinhook (now Paris) in Lamar County — although some believe it was Old Warren, then county seat of Fannin County, or Bois d'Arc, which, that same year, became the *new* county seat and changed its name to Bonham. And regardless of location, there is reason to believe they were never officially married, despite attempts to find someone to legalize the ceremony. In 1844 at least two of their fellow Dallasites said they had only a bond marriage (whereby a couple declares the intention to legally unite when possible), and Margaret herself, in 1905, could only say she was married by the mail rider out of Bonham.

At any rate, Margaret and Neely became Dallas' founding residents. But young Margaret refused to live in his old dugout, so Neely built her a log cabin as a wedding gift of sorts. She made him a pair of beaded moccasins.

Philip Nolan Made Literature

Nearly 200 years ago a mysterious figure in American history named Philip Nolan may have tried to set up an independent nation in the North Texas area we now call the Metroplex. Nolan was a citizen of the new American republic, but after 1790 spent most of his time in French Louisiana or at Nacogdoches, in Spanish Texas.

In 1791 he obtained permission from the Spanish authorities to hunt wild mustangs on the Texas prairies, and during these roundups he lived with the Indians at the future sites of both Dallas and Fort Worth, and came to possess vast information about Spanish frontier lands. Constantly returning to Texas on supposedly innocent business, Nolan aroused the suspicions of the Spanish when they learned he had been granted a private interview by American Vice-President Thomas Jefferson in 1799. An order was issued that Philip Nolan was to be arrested if he entered Texas again. The Spanish believed Nolan planned to use his Indian allies and American adventurers to take over a northern portion of their province and set up a nation. Many American authorities viewed him as a potential traitor to the United States. A protege of General James Wilkinson, the notorious western conspirator, Nolan was believed to be part of Wilkinson's dreams of Southwest empire, independent of the U.S.

In 1801 Nolan was on a contraband horse hunting expedition in North Texas when Spanish troops tried to arrest him. Nolan was killed in a pitched battle — tradition says on Noland River, near Cleburne, although it was probably farther south nearer Waco. The classic 1863 short story, "The Man Without a Country," uses Philip Nolan as its main character, but author Edward Everett Hale denied the historical Nolan was the prototype, and in 1901 wrote *The Real Philip Nolan,* almost in self defense.

Charming Early Names

Early settlers gave their daughters some charming names, although at the time they were not considered unusual or any more "charming" than Mary, Jane, or Sally. Here are a few, gleaned from the Tarrant County census of 1850, that appear unusual to our eyes.

The name Permelia, which showed up in seven of the 79 families listed in that 1850 census, was the most prevalent of the "old fashioned" names. Maj. Ripley Arnold, commandant of newly established Fort Worth, had a daughter born in Florida who was named — Florida. And one of the three Dizannas listed on the census rolls was a daughter of Susanah Foster, whose cabin was the first house in Grapevine.

Farilda was a child of Big John Elliston, the blacksmith at Birdville, first county seat of Tarrant County. Almeda was the name of Richard Crowley's young wife; Didamay Howerton was listed as age 17 and unmarried, but Dosha Ann Foster, age 22, was already a widow. The wife of Middleton Tate Johnson, of Johnson's Station (called father of Tarrant County), was Vreena.

Selete, Seleta, and Salita, were all present on the census rolls — possibly the census taker's misspelling of the same first-name (census takers of that day were not always accurate in their "spelling-by-ear" lists). Archie Leonard, Forth Worth's first storekeeper, had daughters named Selete and Barbesha. In addition to Florida, noted above, we find America, Alabama, and Texana on the census records. And Lucitta, Aramenta, Jebitha and Medora are wives or daughters in White Settlement. One set of triplets is listed: Permelia, Mahulda, and James Neil. Arlalisa and Cimbla Moore were sisters — and while listing other unusual names without comment, the census taker noted that Jephany Porter was female. Aviriah Howerton could be a man's name (in fact, often was, in those times) but the Tarrant County listing is a woman. And there was Mrs. Sevina Lane, who named her sons Camuth and Rocksey — so the female had no monopoly on unusual pioneer names.

Bird's Fort: The Beginning

The first settled spot in the Dallas-Fort Worth area was Bird's Fort, located south of present day Euless in Tarrant County. The fort was built in the fall of 1841 by a group of volunteers under Maj. Jonathan Bird. It was located in the crook of a pretty spring-fed lake which the men called "Lake Sophia," in honor of Col. Holland Coffee's wife, because "it, too, is a heavenly body."

Bird's Fort consisted of a block house with an outer wall of logs and a deep trench surrounding it. An earlier expedition had camped on the site briefly during the summer of 1841, losing one member killed by Indians in what would become Dallas — near Interstate 35E and Regal Row. Bird spent his own money on the fort, and asked the Republic of Texas for compensation, but President Sam Houston turned him down, citing the inability of the Republic "to pay claims and sustain its government" at the same time.

In October 1841 half a dozen Illinois families settled at the newly built fort, hoping to claim land under the Military Road Act, but by 1842 the Republic of Texas had abrogated the act and included the fort area in a Peters Colony grant, so the settlers had to move. That winter, John Neely Bryan, who had helped build Bird's Fort, rode over from his bluff above the Trinity (now in downtown Dallas) and persuaded several of the families, including that of his future wife, Margaret Beeman, to come join him. Thus, Bird's Fort supplied early citizens of Dallas — and one, Charity Gilbert, seems to have supplied Dallas' name.

Bird's Fort was the breaking-up place for the Republic of Texas' ill-fated Snively Expedition to New Mexico in August 1843. In September 1843 it gave its name to an important Texas Indian treaty. By 1845 the fort had become the private property of Samuel Kephart. In 1910 the Bird's Fort earthworks were still visible when Calloway Country Club included the site. In recent years the owners promised a Trinity River levee project would not inundate the historic site.

Dallas' First Taverns

Although Dallas' initial citizen, John Neely Bryan, was generous with the whiskey gourd when visitors appeared, and Adam Haught dispensed wet goods at some point after his arrival in 1845, Dallas didn't get its first tavern until 1846, nearly five years following the founding of the village. That year the Beeman family's Dallas Tavern opened under the management of Henry Harter who was married to Elizabeth Beeman, sister of Bryan's wife, Margaret. Although it was called an inn, its main attraction was its bar. One account says the innkeeper merely shared his bedroom with the travelers. The Dallas Tavern was located at the northwest corner of Houston and Commerce streets, on today's Dealey Plaza.

James Bryan, a brother of John Neely Bryan, married Mrs. Harter (who divorced Henry) and took the tavern over. Then William Beeman, Mrs. Harter-Bryan's brother, affectionately known as Uncle Billy, operated it, claiming in later years that he made it the first true inn. He sold the tavern to Tom Crutchfield who tore it down and in 1852 erected Dallas' first *real* hotel, The Crutchfield House, where everyone had a private bed, if not private rooms.

An 1875 Dallas directory tells of an early tavern competitor, "a Mr. Worth," the colorful description notes, "who supplied the wearied traveler or the bibulous reveler with a passable brand of whiskey at the tent in which his viand was retailed — to recount the festive scenes or compile the crude witticisms that flourished in and around this novel bar-room would be a greater task than the limited space of this narrative will permit." The barrel in early Dallas was apparently never dry.

Some Family Name Creeks

Several creeks in Denton and Tarrant counties were named for unusual reasons — if we accept the statements of certain early day historians.

Between Justin and Roanoke, in southwest Denton County, the modern map shows a series of small streams named Oliver, Harriet, Elizabeth, and Henrietta — along with Trail Creek. E.F. Bates, in his history of Denton County, said all these were named by Oliver Hedgcoxe, agent for the Peters Colony in the 1840s and '50s. Bates says Hedgcoxe, surveying the country, named the creeks in honor of his wife, Elizabeth, and his children. Trail Creek? Trail was the name of his favorite hound.

We may be forgiven some doubt, perhaps, when we discover Bates thought Fossil Creek was named for Hedgcoxe's son Foss, nickname of his son Farseyo.

There are Bear creeks all over Texas, but the one in northeast Tarrant County is different when it comes to the origin of its name. Most Bear creeks, of course, were named for the animal. But Bear Creek in Tarrant County, which formerly flowed through the south end of D/FW Airport, was supposedly named for an early settler who farmed along its course. No, his name wasn't Bear — according to legend, it was B-A-R-C-R-O-F-T. But he pronounced it "Bear-croft". And it didn't take long for his neighbors to turn *"Bear*croft Creek" into Bear Creek — which it is today.

Dallas A Century Ago

A century or so ago the *Texas State Gazeteer* reported Dallas "has never had an epidemic of any kind, is far above the yellow fever level, and with its pure and bracing atmosphere, both summer and winter, is one of the most desirable residence cities in the Union."

By the mid-eighties Dallas had five railroads, the Telephone Company had 40 miles of telephone wire in operation; the Dallas Electric Light Company had just opened, and there were in the city, 2 opera houses, 3 broom factories, 3 street railways, 3 daily papers — the morning *Herald* (not today's *Herald)*, the afternoon *News* (not today's *News)* and the afternoon *Times* — and 11 weeklies, ranging from Norton's *Intelligencer* and the *Texas Volksblatt* to the *Estray Record* for recovering wandering livestock.

Frank Ham owned the Dallas Sausage Factory, George Hamm sold meat, and Dr. Paine was an M.D. Ursuline Academy for young ladies charged $100 per semester for board, washing, stationery, "ordinary infirmary expenses" and tuition, but "Young Ladies desiring admittance into the Academy must always produce satisfactory testimonials."

Sanger Bros. was at 510 Main (now El Centro College); Wm. Weston Hardware was next door to Charles Ott, gunsmith, on Elm Street (the Ott building was standing a century later); J.E. Flanders, architect, advertised he had designed courthouses for six Texas counties, including Dallas (that one burned in 1890); and familiar family names are sprinkled through the 1884-85 directory, such as Akin, Aldridge, Benners, Coombes, Gano, Kahn, Schoellkopf, Prather, Seay, Stemmons, Spence, and Rick.

A prophetic editor wrote: "The possibilities of Dallas can only be partially anticipated from her marvelous advancement since her real progress began, but is certain that she is as yet only on the threshold of a glorious career, which shall at no distant date astonish not only the inhabitants of Texas but the whole civilized world."

A Pioneer Feminist

Among the Norwegian immigrants who settled in Kaufman County in the 1840s, none was so famous in Europe as beautiful Elise Waerenskjold, editor, author, and very much a liberated woman.

Daughter of a Lutheran minister, Elise was educated by tutors, and at age 19 became a teacher — a rare step for Scandinavian women at the time. She is still remembered in Norwegian history as a women's rights leader. In 1839, at age 24, she married a young sea captain, Svend Foyn, who today is honored as founder of the Norwegian whaling industry and who became quite wealthy. Their marriage, however, ended in amicable separation.

When Elise's friends Johan Reiersen and wife Christian left Norway for Texas, Elise became editor of the Reiersens' magazine, *Norge og Amerika (Norway and America),* and in 1847 she, too, emigrated to Texas, where, to the scandal of the colony, the next year, she married Wilhelm Waerenskjold six months before her divorce from Foyn was final. She and Wilhelm settled at Four-Mile Prairie in Kaufman County where a number of Norwegians were living, and Wilhelm went into milling and contracting. For 45 years her letters and other publications were not only a great incentive to Norwegian immigration to America, but remain a valuable observation on pioneer life in North Texas.

In 1866, though the Civil War was over, Wilhelm was murdered because of his opposition to slavery, and Elise had to support herself and children for years through her sales ingenuity as well as her pen. Although she paid little attention to American politics, other than to have opposed slavery, she continued her belief in freedom of women. She finally had to ask financial aid from her first husband, who gladly gave it.

She died at Hamilton, Texas in 1895, far better known in her native country than in the United States, and only in recent years has her importance to Texas history been recognized.

Dallas Had A Gold Rush

In December 1848, United States President James K. Polk officially announced the discovery of gold in California, displaying 230 ounces of the stuff and starting an international stampede. Within weeks, thousands of "Forty-niners" were heading for the West Coast. As rumors of fabulous wealth swept the nation, more and more of the westbound travelers made their way through Dallas County, most of them using California Crossing, located a few miles up the Elm Fork of the Trinity from what was then the center of the town. (That's the way the modern street got its name.)

The frontier village wasn't immune to gold fever, of course, and lots of Dallas men joined the rush. John Neely Bryan, the father and promoter of Dallas, took off in 1850 to look for gold, leaving his wife Margaret to sell his Dallas real estate. John C. McCoy, a young lawyer who had come to Dallas as a Peters Colony agent, joked that he was the only male remaining in town.

But within a few months of President Polk's official announcement, Dallas had its own gold rush. In August of 1849, fired by "secret" geological reports, some 80 inhabitants of Dallas and Tarrant counties are reported to have taken off to pan the waters and prospect the mountains of — Oklahoma. The gold-seekers staged their "rush" to the present vicinity of Ardmore, Oklahoma, and from there searched the Arbuckle and Wichita mountains for glitter, evidence of which was supposedly abundant. Two months later, having avoided encounters with the Comanche and Kiowa Indians only because an Asiatic cholera epidemic was raging among the tribes, the Dallas goldseekers came dragging home, gold-less, and glad to be back.

The New 1850 Jail

In November 1850, Dallas County decided it needed a real jail instead of the flimsy shed lawbreakers were being kept in. Specifications were issued and bids were asked for the construction. The foundation of the new jail was to be of cedar posts, set on end and shaved down to a point so as to be driven into the earth and form a wall. The floors were to be of oak timber 10 inches thick. An *inside* wall similar to the *outside* wall was to be built, and the space between the two filled with timbers eight inches thick — for a total wall thickness of 24 inches.

The ceiling was to be of oak, 10 inches thick, and the roof of hand-rived shingles, "well nailed on," and the gable ends weather-boarded up "with well-shaved boards or planks." The door was to be 3½ feet wide and five feet high, of oak planks six inches thick with large iron spikes securing them. Two shutters on the door were to have a 10-penny nail "driven in every square inch on each side of each shutter."

This grim little 16 x 16 foot structure was to have windows 10 x 16 inches, "cased up with slab iron wide enough to fasten to each wall and spiked strongly to same with two wide iron bars passing horizontally across the window and 3¼ inch-square iron bars placed perpendicularly passing through the horizontal bars." No provision was made for heat or for any other light.

The jail, on one side of the courthouse square, was finished in May 1851, and 21 Dallas citizens assumed personal notes to pay the $830.20 that the building cost.

The Important Texas Towns

When Dallas and Fort Worth were first growing up, they weren't very important. In the 1840s, Lancaster was as big as Dallas, and Farmers Branch was better known. Fort Inglish (Bonham) in Fannin County, for years was the nearest seat of government to Dallas, and Preston, at the Red River crossing near Holland Coffee's trading post was busier.

The Peters Colony, which drew hundreds of settlers to the Dallas-Fort Worth region, had its local office at Stewartsville, in Denton County (there's still a creek named "Office Branch" running into Lake Lewisville), and Bazette, Trinidad, and Magnolia, on the Trinity River below Dallas County, had steamboats calling regularly, while Dallas was limited in its use of the river to a few ferries. Birdville was the first county seat of Tarrant County and had both a courthouse and two newspapers before Fort Worth had either.

Black Jack Grove, to the east, was the rendezvous point and jumping off place for westward freight wagons in the 1850s. And in the case of Fort Worth, it looked for sure that Weatherford, 20 miles west, would far outdistance it during the 1850s and '60s.

Marshall, financial capital of East Texas, in 1870 was headquarters for the Southern Transcontinental Railroad (Texas & Pacific) while neither Dallas nor Fort Worth had a railroad, and nearby Jefferson, via Caddo Lake, was the second biggest port in Texas and richer and more cosmopolitan even than Marshall. Practically everything Dallas bought in those days had to come through Jefferson.

Clarksville, up on the Red River, was older than Dallas and was the educational center for all of North Texas with its renowned college, McKenzie Institute. Even after the Civil War, Clarksville's newspaper, *The Northern Standard,* was the most important publication in the north half of the state.

Galveston was the biggest, richest most fashionable city in Texas and looked down her nose at upstart villages like Dallas, Fort Worth and Houston.

Texas, Our Texas

Ask most non-Texans what the Texas state song is and they will almost invariably guess, "The Eyes of Texas." But as anyone who has gone through the Texas school system knows, such is not the case. The official State Song of Texas is "Texas, Our Texas."

"The Eyes of Texas" is the official song of the University of Texas at Austin, the words written in 1903 — to the tune of the old folk song, "I've Been Workin' on the Railroad" — by a student for a campus minstrel show, poking good natured fun at U.T. President William Prather who constantly exhorted the students: "Remember, the eyes of Texas are on you!" When Prather died in 1905 the song was sung as a tribute by students at his funeral, thus beginning its recognition as the school song.

Interestingly enough, "Texas, Our Texas" was written by an Englishman — William John Marsh. Born in Liverpool in 1880, Marsh came to Texas in 1904 after training as a composer and organist. He was made professor of organ, composition, and music theory at Texas Christian University. In 1917 he became a naturalized citizen of the United States.

"Texas, Our Texas," came about in 1918 after a friend suggested to Gladys Yoakum Wright, a Greenville native then living in Fort Worth, that she show some of her lyrics to Marsh, who, she was told, "writes beautiful music." Marsh composed the music and together with Mrs. Wright produced the words. In 1923 Gov. Pat Neff offered a prize of $1,000 for a state song and 286 compositions were submitted. "Texas, Our Texas" won the prize. It was adopted by the 41st legislature in 1929 and made official state song in a formal ceremony on March 11, 1930.

Since then, three generations of Texas school children have learned to pipe the Lone Star anthem . . . "Texas, our Texas, all hail the mighty state!"

P. KOLSTP

Cynthia Ann Parker

Cynthia Ann Parker, the most famous Texas Indian captive, was taken with her 6-year-old brother John in a Comanche raid on Fort Parker, in Limestone County, May 19, 1836 when she was nine years old. Given the name Preloch, she grew up with the tribe and eventually became wife of Chief Peta Nocona and mother of Quanah Parker, the last Comanche war chief, and Pecos, whom history has lost. Her brother John also became Indianized, but married a Mexican girl, left the tribe and became a rancher. He served in the little-known Mexican Confederate company during the American Civil War, but returned to Mexico where he died in 1915.

Cynthia Ann and a 2-year-old daughter, Topasannah or Prairie Flower, were recaptured in 1860 by Texas Rangers in a battle on Pease River, in Foard County, in which Peta Nocona was reported killed. Identified by her uncle, Isaac Parker, Cynthia Ann and her baby were taken to Birdville, near Fort Worth, to live. James "Coho" Smith, a Dallas-Tarrant County pioneer, was brought in to translate for her — she had forgotten English, save her name — and as they conversed in Indian dialect, she offered Smith chieftain status if he would help her escape back to her tribe. Some of the other men who were present grew suspicious, and warned Smith not to engage in "so much gibberish."

A famous portrait of Cynthia Ann nursing Prairie Flower was taken at a Fort Worth daguerreotype gallery in 1862. Although the 1861 Texas Legislature voted her 4,400 acres of land, plus a pension, she could not be reconciled to the white world and tried to flee throughout the first year of her return to its fold.

She lived in Van Zandt, then Anderson counties with her brother, Silas, Jr., who had been appointed her guardian. Topasannah died in 1864 and Cynthia Ann pined away a few months later. In 1910 she and her child were reburied at Cache, Oklahoma, among her chosen Comanche people, but in 1956, she, Quanah, and Topasannah were again reburied in the Army cemetery at Fort Sill, Okla.

Captain Gilbert's Journey

Dallas owes much to a man with what sounds like a woman's name — Capt. Mabel Gilbert. Mabel (a family name pronounced MAY-bell) Gilbert was a riverboat captain who moved to Fannin County in 1837, joined by his family, which then numbered eight children. In the fall of 1841, Gilbert and his wife, Charity Morris Gilbert, located at Bird's Fort, south of Euless, which he had helped construct. Appropriately, in March 1842, when the riverboat captain decided to join John Neely Bryan at his proposed townsite on a Trinity River bluff, Gilbert and his wife floated down the river on a two-log raft the captain had had built.

Charity Gilbert was thus the first white female citizen of what became Dallas. She brought the first black, a young slave named Smith who had been reared like a son, and she more than likely gave birth to the first white child born in Dallas. She was pregnant at the time of their raft trip in 1842, and the 1850 census shows a ninth Gilbert child, Morris, as being eight years old. There's evidence she also suggested the name Dallas, in honor of Commodore Alexander James Dallas, a prominent United States naval officer and a good friend of the Morris and Gilbert families.

The Gilberts didn't bring their family on the raft. The younger children came later with Wilson Gilbert, Mabel's brother who was also a river captain. Bryan was particularly anxious to get Capt. Gilbert to Dallas because Bryan wanted his expertise in promoting his city as a river port.

Mabel Gilbert and his wife lived in a cabin which Bryan and some others had built for them — the first house in Dallas. The Gilberts farmed at a spring across the river from Bryan, near Commerce and Industrial streets. They left Dallas in 1844, giving up their land — which today would be worth millions. Later Gilbert pioneered Wichita County. Charity died, after her tenth child, and Capt. Gilbert married again, fathering his nineteenth offspring at age 73. Numerous descendents remain in North Texas.

The Chisholm Trail

Jesse Chisholm started Fort Worth to being "Cowtown," but he probably never saw the place. Chisholm, of Scottish and Cherokee ancestry, migrated with the Cherokees from Tennessee to Arkansas, and later had a trading post at Council Grove on the North Canadian River near present day Oklahoma City. His freight wagons had cut a 220-mile path from Wichita, Kansas down to his store, and in 1866, when a Texas cattleman asked about the best way to drive a herd to the Kansas market, he was advised to "take Chisholm's trail."

By 1868, thanks to the promotion of Joseph G. McCoy, hired by the developers of Abilene, Kansas, to get a trail laid out to bring Texas herds to their railhead, the entire cattle trail from South Texas to Kansas was called the Chisholm Trail. Those Chisholm Trail cattle drives of story, song, and film went through Fort Worth, heading north up Main Street, crossing the Trinity River "under the bluff" and continuing through Denton and Cooke counties.

Fort Worth was where the several Texas branches of the Trail came together and where trail drivers outfitted their cowboys for the long trip across the Indian Nations. In season, the Trail was a living, animal river. In 1871 half a million head of cattle passed through Fort Worth going up the Chisholm Trail. The Trail was the beginning of the historic connection between Fort Worth and the cattle industry. Although later trails were westward, Fort Worth remained "Cowtown" in the hearts and minds of Texas forever more, by 1905 becoming the third largest beef packing center in the United States.

Poor Jesse Chisholm died in 1868 from eating tainted bear meat from a copper pot, never dreaming how celebrated his name would become.

Merrell Cemetery

There were dozens of small, private cemeteries in the Dallas and Fort Worth area, begun by pioneer families, or left from churches that have disappeared with time. Some, such as the White Rock resting place of Warren Angus Ferris, the region's first surveyor, are said to have vanished beneath apartment complexes, parking lots, or tennis courts. Many, like the Mooneyham Cemetery, off Webb Chapel Road in northwest Dallas, have been vandalized almost out of existence, and certain Arlington area burial grounds acquired an unfortunate ghostly reputation, leading to their near-destruction. Even famous Pioneer Rest Cemetery, near the Dallas Convention Center, suffers from too much public exposure. The graves of many historical figures in Dallas and Tarrant counties have been lost through such neglect, or callous disregard.

A pleasant exception, still in use, is the Merrell Cemetery, in northwest Dallas, on Merrell Road west of Midway, on land originally furnished by Benjamin Merrell, first tax assessor of Dallas County. Tall native trees shelter this well kept resting place, and the headstones read like a chapter in early Dallas history — or a street map of the area. Here you find buried the Straits of Strait Lane, the Welches and Coxes of Welch and Cox lanes, the Rossers of Rosser Road, the Coppedges of Coppedge Lane — and, of course, several Merrells of Merrell Road. Numbers of descendents of these families remain in Dallas County, most of them active in the cemetery association.

The first marked burial was that of Elder Eli Merrell in 1849. A Disciples of Christ preacher, this patriarch of the Merrell clan brought them here in 1844 as Peters Colonists. The first Straits, William and Mourning, lived on Seven-Mile Road (now Walnut Hill), and Strait Lane, in the 19th century, was merely the path from their house up to their sons' farms.

Although vandals forced the cemetery association to lock the gate, the Merrell Cemetery remains a beautiful haven surrounded by homes.

Rosendahl, The Dirigible Man

Following World War I the United States Navy began building giant dirigible airships, fashioned after the German Zeppelins. For lifting power, the U.S. airships used non-explosive helium gas, produced at Fort Worth.

The first Navy airship was the *Shenandoah,* launched in 1923, which was wrecked with loss of many lives in a 1925 windstorm. But a group of Navy officers insisted airships were valuable and safe — pointing to the success of the Zeppelins, none of which had crashed in years of voyaging. One of these officers was Lieutenant Commander Charles Rosendahl, of Cleburne, Texas, who had moved to Cleburne as a boy when his father was transferred there by the Santa Fe Railroad. Rosendahl attended high school in Cleburne and received his Naval Academy appointment from the Cleburne congressional district. His wife was also from Texas. When the Navy's new airship, *Akron,* was christened, Rosendahl was picked to command her first transcontinental flight in May 1932.

The *Akron* was 785 feet long and 135 feet in diameter, carrying 6.5 million cubic feet of gas — the largest airship flown to that time. Five airplanes operated from her by means of hooks. Virtually all North Texas turned out as the *Akron* flew over Fort Worth and down to Cleburne, dipping low over Rosendahl's hometown. The non-stop flight from Lakehurst, N.J., center of East Coast airship operations, to San Diego, took only 27 hours, creating a national sensation.

But later the *Akron* went down, taking Admiral William Moffett, the Navy's aeronautics chief, to death with it, and then her sister ship, the *Macon,* crashed, ending the Navy's dirigible era. Commander Rosendahl, who was not aboard in these disasters (most authorities believe he could have averted the loss of the *Akron* had he been in command), was the last high-ranking Navy lighter-than-air officer. He died May 17, 1977 at Lakehurst. His lighter-than-air collection is housed at the University of Texas at Dallas as part of its famous aviation library.

Cumberland Hill

Cumberland Hill was a prominent elevation north of the village of Dallas which attracted picnickers and lovers in the days before the Civil War. Located in the general area of the modern Fairmont Hotel and Woodall Rogers Freeway, and crossed by Akard Street, the hill got its name when an early day Cumberland Presbyterian congregation built a small frame schoolhouse on its summit. The first Union troops to arrive in Dallas after the Civil War camped on Cumberland Hill, in December 1865, and a few years later, the Dallas City Gas Light Company erected a huge gas storage tank near the site.

In 1879 the fabled Dallas *grand dame,* Mrs. Jules (Belle) Schneider, and her husband erected the first of the Ross Avenue mansions on the northeast corner of Ross and Akard, on Cumberland Hill. Akard Street, at that point, was Belle's private driveway. Belle Schneider kept a private orchestra to play for her dances and her home is said to have had three kitchens for the simultaneous preparation of three different types of meals.

One of the first public schools in Dallas was built on Cumberland Hill in 1888, replacing the little Presbyterian building, which was moved a few blocks away to serve as a black school. The big new brick edifice was named, fittingly, Cumberland Hill School. At one time it was the most socially acceptable school in town, and it was said that the carriages delivering children to school rivaled, in number and splendor, those that delivered debutantes to the famous Idlewild ball. Jesse Jones, noted Houston financier, attended Cumberland Hill School when his parents lived in Dallas. Cumberland Hill School was used by generations of Dallas students until the 1960s.

In 1970 the building was sold to Sedco, Inc., an oil drilling firm headed by former Texas Gov. Bill Clements. Clements, whose family was associated with Cumberland Hill School, persuaded his company to restore the old school building to its early grandeur, and today it is international headquarters for the company.

P. KOLSTI

P. KOLSTI

Pioneer Heroine

Amanda Jane Crawford was two years old when her family moved to the Flower Mound community in Denton County in 1855. In 1873 she married John M. Raines, a young man in that pioneering community, and they raised six children. Amanda Jane Raines would have been a mere name on a list of early settlers had it not been for an unfortunate occurrence in her childhood. When she was six years old, the little girl was stricken with polio. She was never able to walk or use her feet again.

For a 19th century farm child, the handicap would have seemed insurmountable, but not for Amanda Jane. As a youngster she learned to do housework on her hands and knees, sharing in all the difficult labor of a frontier farm home: she literally scooted in her work. She attended school by means of a specially built box hitched to her pony, which she drove by herself. We are not told of her and John Raines' courtship, but she must have been a lively and attractive woman. The very fact that no one seemed to recall she had a disability is witness to that. After she married, to make her family's clothes, she disconnected the treadle so she could operate a sewing machine with one hand and guide the cloth with the other. She drove her six children wherever they needed to go, becoming an expert with wagons and buggies. She did her share of church and community work, too, and all without having any hired help.

Amanda Jane died in 1949, nearing the age of 95. Her surviving children agreed nothing had kept her from leading a full life — but *they* placed more emphasis than *she* did on something that happened on her 50th birthday. On that occasion, after half a century of scooting around on hands and knees, Amanda Jane Crawford Raines became the owner of a wheel chair.

Dallas Landowners

A century ago — who were the big landowners of Dallas County? Well, not too surprisingly perhaps, according to the *Texas Gazetteer,* a 19th century commercial directory, the *biggest* Dallas landowner at that time was William Caruth, with 5,816 acres scattered over the county, but mainly in what is now North Dallas. His brother Walter, with 3,284 acres, was the No. 3 landowner. William and Walter's land firm was named "W. Caruth & Bro." which assured that neither brother would be construed as the other's boss. That's the same Caruth family that still holds much valuable Dallas County land.

The second largest 1883 landowner was John H. (Uncle Jack) Cole whose 4,336 acres would be worth untold millions today because much of the land became the choicest part of Old Highland Park. Cole Avenue was named for him and his family.

The fourth largest landowner was John C. McCoy whose 3,417 acres included the campus of today's Hockaday School for girls. John C. McCoy, who came to Dallas in 1845, was the city's first lawyer. Widow Sarah Cockrell's 3,144 acres, next in size, were strategically located in downtown Dallas and southwest Dallas County, and helped make her the city's first female millionaire.

Other major landowners of the mid-1880s were: J.C. Reed of Grand Prairie, Mrs. E.F. Parker, and Mary Matley and sons — each owning about 2,500 acres. W.H. Thomas's 2,335 acres included one large area known as the Thomas Ranch — one of the few places officially called a ranch in Dallas County. Crawford Treese (or Trees), whose marriage to Annie Henderson in 1846 was the first in newly organized Dallas County, was the tenth biggest landowner with nearly 2,000 acres around Cedar Hill.

Cotton Bowl in Fair Park

Although the Cotton Bowl at Fair Park is famous for its annual New Year's Day game and the Texas-Oklahoma grudge match during the State Fair of Texas, football was featured at Fair Park long before there was a Cotton Bowl Classic or a Texas-OU Weekend. When the city of Dallas purchased the fair grounds from the State Fair Association in 1904, a football field was already in use, renting for $25 per game. And "field" was all it was — mainly dirt cleared of rocks.

Athletic facilities were expanded in 1914 when Fair Park took over Gaston Park (about where the Music Hall stands today), which contained a small stadium that had once served as home field for the Dallas Giants of the Texas League. The first Texas-OU game in Dallas, with both as Southwest Conference members, was played Oct. 19, 1918. The Southwest Conference had been organized in Dallas in 1914 with the support of State Fair members. For several years in the 1920s the game played by the University of Texas at the State Fair was against Vanderbilt, not Oklahoma. The modern Texas-OU series began in 1929.

After World War I, many area colleges and universities began scheduling contests at Fair Park field, and in 1921 a real football stadium was built, with wooden stands seating 13,500, about where the roller coaster runs today. It was razed in 1930 and a magnificent stadium for 45,500 was built on the site of the race track and grandstand. It carried the unimaginative name of Fair Park Stadium.

The first Cotton Bowl game was played there January 1, 1937, Texas Christian University defeating Marquette 16-6. By the time the Southwest Conference took over as host team in 1941, Fair Park Stadium itself had become The Cotton Bowl. In 1948 the west side was doubledecked and during 1949 the east side was doubledecked to enlarge the Cotton Bowl to 75,500 seats (its present size) for the 1950 game.

The first Cotton Bowl game to be televised was in 1953 when Texas beat Tennessee 16-0.

Garland Was Duck Creek

Garland was originally Duck Creek and was located on the west bank of that creek, on the road from Dallas to Greenville (now Garland Road). The site was about a mile west of today's downtown Garland. Duck Creek school had been built as early as 1858, and three stores and two grist mills were operating in the village in the 1870s. Duck Creek was granted a post office in 1878.

In 1886 the Katy railroad built through the area from Greenville to Dallas, and a short time later the Santa Fe railroad crossed the Katy from the south, going from Dallas to Greenville. Both railroads missed the village of Duck Creek, however, so various citizens laid out two new towns — one near the Santa Fe depot was named Embree, after Postmaster K.H. Embree, and one near the Katy depot assumed the proud title of New Duck Creek. The hamlets refused to join hands, but in 1887 a fire wiped out most of the original Duck Creek, at which time New Duck Creek claimed the post office — but Embree contested it. The rivalry was settled in 1888 when newly-elected Congressman Jo Abbott, at the suggestion of Thomas F. Nash, got the post office department to relocate the post office halfway between New Duck Creek and Embree, naming it Garland, to honor President Grover Cleveland's attorney General, A.H. Garland, who had earlier been a Confederate congressman from Tennessee.

Garland was first incorporated in 1891 and in 1899 a fire gutted the business district, causing it to be rebuilt in brick around the square that is still the heart of the city. Garland modernized its charter on November 4, 1913, which marks its true municipal birthday. It remained a small country town until after World War II, when it burst its seams. Today with 145,000 residents Garland is one of the state's larger cities and is the second largest in Dallas County.

P. KOLSTØ

Dealey Plaza

Dealey Plaza, in downtown Dallas, scene of the assassination of President John F. Kennedy, is also the birthplace of the City of Dallas. John Neely Bryan, founder of Dallas, had his first home, a dugout, there and drew off plans for his city. Bryan's dugout was located very near the spot where President Kennedy was hit by sniper bullets. The plaza was created when the Triple Underpass was built in 1935, combining the lower ends of Elm, Main and Commerce streets into West Commerce. It was named for George Bannerman Dealey, publisher of the *Dallas Morning News,* honoring him as "father of city planning" in Dallas. A statue of Robert E. Lee was intended for Dealey Plaza, but that monument was shifted to Oak Lawn Park and the park's name changed to Lee Park. The statue of Dealey, in Dealey Plaza, was erected in 1949, after his death in 1946.

The area included in Dealey Plaza — some 3 acres — is the historical heart of the city. It entered history in 1837 before there was a thought of Dallas, when a group of Texas frontier fighters, fleeing down the Elm Fork of the Trinity from a disastrous encounter with Indians, reached the spot safely. The Kickapoo Trace, an Indian highway, crossed the river nearby.

In 1841, when Bryan arrived, the plaza site was on an 18-foot bluff overlooking the Trinity River, which was moved a mile west in the late 1920s. The Triple Underpass is constructed on the former riverbed. The south end (Commerce extension) of the underpass was the site of the first wooden bridge (1855) and the first iron bridge (1872) over the Trinity, both owned by Sarah Horton Cockrell.

For many years Water and Broadway streets paralleled Houston Street to the west at the Dealey Plaza site, and the first stagecoach station in Dallas was at Main and Broadway. Both streets disappeared when the Triple Underpass was built. Dallas' first real hotel, the Crutchfield House, stood at the northwest corner of Houston and Main.

Quanah Parker

Quanah Parker was a son of Chief Peta Nocona and Cynthia Ann Parker, the famous white captive. The last Comanche war chief, Quanah became a shrewd businessman after he led the remnants of his tribe onto an Oklahoma reservation in 1875. (Parker County is named for Cynthia Ann's family, the town of Nocona for her husband, and Quanah for her son.)

Chief Quanah was often in Fort Worth conferring with ranchers about leasing tribal lands for grazing, and in 1885 civilization almost got him where the U.S. Cavalry had failed. Parker and his uncle, Yellow Bear, were in Fort Worth to discuss some overdue rents with an Indian agent. The Indian men registered at the Pickwick, Fort Worth's finest hotel, and Yellow Bear retired early while Quanah went to spend some time with the foreman of the Waggoner Ranch, one of the lessees. Quanah returned to the hotel room after two hours and also went to bed. Thirteen hours later the two were found in their room — Yellow Bear dead and Quanah Parker unconscious and near death.

First newspaper accounts claimed Quanah had blown out the gaslight instead of turning off the gas. It was presumed a reservation Indian wouldn't know about modern wonders. But Quanah had visited Washington and other large cities and was familiar with such facilities. When he later regained consciousness he said he had not blown out the gaslight, but in turning off the gas had failed to close the jet completely, allowing deadly fumes to fill the room. Quanah slept near a partially opened window, which saved his life.

The erroneous story of his blowing out the gas was circulated as fact for over eighty years, until Ron Tyler, a Fort Worth historian, took the trouble to read the next issues of the Fort Worth newspaper following the tragedy and discovered Quanah Parker's statement. Chief Quanah continued to be a frequent Fort Worth visitor — always in electrically lighted hotels, however — until his death in 1911.

P. KOLSTI

Highland Park Named
for A Horse Farm

In 1889 a group of eastern financiers put together the biggest single deal in suburban real estate ever made in Texas, paying half a million dollars for 1,300 acres of land along Turtle Creek north of Dallas. The project was called Philadelphia Place because the City of Brotherly Love was where most of the money came from.

Col. Henry Exall, who was put in charge of development, built graveled streets and put a dam across Turtle Creek to create Exall Lake, but the Panic of 1893 stopped Philadelphia Place, and for the next 13 years Exall operated a horse farm called Lomo Alto on part of the acreage. Lomo Alto Street leads from Lemmon Avenue to where his breeding farm was, north of Mockingbird Lane. Exall's horses were famous in racing circles and he often took top purses at the State Fair of Texas.

Exall Lake, lying immediately south of Beverly Drive, between Preston Road and Lakeside, was a popular picnic and boating spot for Dallas for many years. The North Dallas Railway, a streetcar line, went out McKinney and Cole through what is now Highland Park to Exall Lake. Although the route normally ended at the M-K-T Railroad and Knox Street, if as many as 10 persons wanted to ride to the lake the motorman would make the extra run.

Then in 1906 John S. Armstrong, who had been initially involved with Thomas Marsalis in the development of Oak Cliff, bought the Philadelphia Place land, and with his sons-in-law Edgar Flippen and Hugh Prather, began creating a model community. The partners didn't want to use the old name, which had come to have connotations of failure, so they adapted the name of Exall's horse farm, Lomo Alto, which in Spanish means a piece of high ground. Armstrong and his sons-in-law therefore christened the new suburb Highland Park. The name has proved to be a long-running success.

Texas Independence Day

March 2 is Texas Independence Day, but thousands of Texas residents do not know what brought it about. Despite the fact that March 2 is celebrated, March 3, 1836 was the date the Declaration of Independence was signed by the convention of delegates meeting in Byars & Mercer's new and unfinished building at the town of Washington, now Washington-on-the-Brazos. (The building is usually referred to as a blacksmith or gunsmith shop, but it was neither.) Richard Ellis, for whom Ellis County was named, served as president of the convention, and the declaration was written by George C. Childress, for whom Childress County was named.

The Texas Declaration sets out obligations of a government and certain rights of citizens, then lists grievances against the Mexican government and makes the summary: "We, therefore . . . do hereby resolve and declare that our political connection with the Mexican nation has forever ended; and that the people of Texas do now constitute a free, sovereign and independent republic . . ."

The document was eventually signed by 60 men, including Sam Houston and Sam Maverick. But Stephen F. Austin, the "Father of Texas," was in the United States raising money for the revolutionists. Three Mexican natives are included among the signers.

Texas' independence was not gained until the Battle of San Jacinto, on April 21, 1836, and March 3, the day of the signing, saw the final countdown for the Texan garrison at the Alamo — so the Declaration of Independence could hardly have been made at a more inauspicious time.

Five copies of the Declaration, dispatched to various Texas localities, disappeared. The original was sent to the U.S. Department of State in Washington, D.C. where it remained until 1896, when it was returned to Texas. A photographic copy is on display in the Texas capitol.

Belle Starr

Belle Starr, the legendary "Bandit Queen," made Dallas her home for many years. She was born Myra Maybelle Shirley. At age 16, during the Civil War, she and her family fled Missouri and settled at Scyene, east of Dallas. The Shirleys were a respectable family but two sons (one killed by Federal troops) had been part of Quantrill's guerrillas, and their Scyene home was a haven for former Quantrill outlaws, including Cole and John Younger and Frank and (reportedly) Jesse James.

Legend says Myra married Jim Reed — another outlaw — because he killed the slayer of her twin brother, Ed. The marriage record, recently found in Collin County by Mrs. Alice Pitts, shows "Mira M. Shirley" married to James C. Reed on Nov. 1, 1866 by the Rev. S.M. Wilkins. However, her first child, Pearl, was rumored to be Cole Younger's. Myra apparently used that name during her entire stay in Dallas. Two indictments in Dallas County are against Myra Reed, and a deed filed from Eliza Shirley, her mother, is to Myra M. Reed.

Better educated than most women at the time, Myra once taught school at Scyene. She is said to have shocked Dallas, gambling with the men in bars and, expert horsewoman that she was, racing around town in pants. She and Jim ran a livery stable on Camp Street, near where the *Dallas Times Herald* is today, and may have dealt in stolen horses. Reed was killed in 1874 by a lawman in Lamar County and Belle next became wife of Sam Starr, a Cherokee Indian and member of the notorious Starr Gang. Belle, on Canadian River land Sam inherited, set up a "robbers roost" named Younger Bend. Sam died in a shootout, and Belle had other "husbands," but kept the Starr name, reportedly making the others change theirs.

Most of the colorful stories about Belle are myths. Despite her reputation, she only served time for one crime: serving whiskey in the Indian Nation. She was killed from ambush in 1889 at her home, possibly by her outlaw son Ed, who mistook her for a man. Her only daughter Pearl (who went by Younger) operated the most famous bawdy house in Fort Smith, Arkansas, until a few years before her death in 1925.

Carrollton

The city of Carrollton was begun in 1872 when the Dallas & Wichita Railroad (now the MKT branch to Denton) built as far as the northwest corner of Dallas County and then stopped, out of money. The D&W railroad was an all-Dallas project. Aging John Neely Bryan had turned the first shovelful of dirt for it, but for a few years it looked as though the railroad would never make it out of Dallas County. By 1878, when track-laying resumed, the D&W had gotten no farther than a tree stump near Lewisville. It never did get to Wichita Falls, its announced goal.

The town of Carrollton was laid off by A.W. Perry, who sold lots and gave land for the D&W depot. Perry and W.H. Witt had earlier built the village of Trinity Mills, a few miles north of Carrollton, and for years there was great rivalry between the neighboring towns. Trinity Mills, for example, boasted of having an electrician as early as 1883. The Carrollton-Trinity Mills area was part of the Peters Colony, and the first Baptist church in Dallas County was organized east of present day Carrollton in 1846 by the Rev. David Myers, a colonist from Kentucky.

There is much controversy over Carrollton's name. The Myers family, original landowners in the vicinity, said it was named for the Illinois town where J.M. Myers (a son of the Rev. Myers) originated. J.M. Myers was the first postmaster, so this idea has weight. However, others believe Carrollton was named for Joseph Carroll, an official of the Peters Colony, or George Carroll, a settler from Carrollton, Maryland.

In later years, the Cotton Belt and two sections of the Frisco railroads were built through Carrollton, making it an important rail shipping point for North Texas. And from October 1924 until March 1932, Carrollton was on the Dallas-Denton line of the now-forgotten Texas Interurban Railway. The city's greatest growth came after 1950 when it became a major manufacturing and distribution center. Carrollton today is a flourishing suburban city that has preserved both rural flavor and modern individuality.

Dallas' First Insurance Company

The Modern Order of Praetorians, founded in 1898, was the first of the many life insurance companies to be chartered in Dallas and Texas. This fraternal order was the brainchild of C.B. Gardner, an Illinois native who had come to Dallas in 1895 in the wholesale book business. The Praetorians organization came out of a meeting in the old Oriental Hotel between Gardner, Louis Blaylock, a prominent religious publisher, commercial printer and Masonic leader, and George G. Taylor, another Illinois native, of English parentage, who was only 18 at the time but had worked in the Dallas office of a New York life insurance company since age 16.

Chartered April 1898, the company began operation the first of January, 1899. At the end of the first year the Praetorians had assets of only $49.36, and Blaylock, who later was Police Commissioner and Mayor of Dallas, vowed to pay death claims out of his own pocket. But by 1901 the fraternal order was bold enough to announce plans to construct a 15-story home office building. Excavation began at Main and Stone but much to the Praetorians' chagrin, and the town's amusement, it remained a deep hole in the ground called "Gardner's Folly" for several years. However, when it opened in 1909, the Praetorian Building was the tallest west of the Mississippi and was Dallas' first true skyscraper — and the city's proudest observation tower. In 1960 the Praetorian Building was completely rebuilt, adding another story. It remains a downtown landmark. In 1958 the Praetorian fraternal society was converted to a mutual, legal reserve life insurance company named Praetorian Mutual Life.

Following the Praetorians' success, dozens of insurance companies were chartered in Dallas within a few years. The formation of this insurance company was of great significance to Dallas, because it was the beginning of the city's importance as a financial center, liberating the local economy from dependence on "foreign" investments as well as agriculture or natural resources with their unpredictable cycles of good and bad income.

Pianos in The Metroplex

On the Texas frontier, pianos were more than mere musical instruments. They were a mark of culture, evidence that a village had come of age, almost the equal today of a local symphony orchestra. If someone went to the trouble and expense of pulling and tugging a huge and heavy musical instrument by horse or ox-wagon out to nowhere, it was a sure-enough sign of artistic sincerity.

Dallas got its first piano in 1849 when J. Wellington Latimer came to town to begin the first newspaper, *The Cedar Snag.* His wife, a music teacher, brought her big square piano in the wagon along with her husband's type case and hand-press, and as the implements were being unloaded on the northeast corner of the square, the Dallas townspeople watching the arrival demanded, and got, an impromptu open-air piano concert from Mrs. Latimer there on the square. Editor "Weck" Latimer was very popular, but was killed in a fall in 1859. His widow never seemed to get over her husband's death and became tragically unstable, refusing to touch her piano.

At Fort Worth, the wife of Major Ripley Arnold, the first commandant, is said to have brought her piano out to the military post when it was in operation, but the first piano in the civilian village of Fort Worth was owned by the wife of Dr. M.L. Woods who arrived from Jefferson and moved into the abandoned fort commissary in December 1853, in time for Mrs. Woods to play Christmas carols for the handful of settlers who had taken over the empty military buildings.

Some Indians were reported to have seen the piano being unloaded and decided the keys were the teeth of a strange animal that had to be hit to be made to sing. After overcoming their initial fears, the Indians, on other visits to Fort Worth, were said to have approached the Woods' dwelling, appealing to Mrs. Woods and her piano-playing daughters, "Peck, gals, peck," while they stood on the front porch to listen.

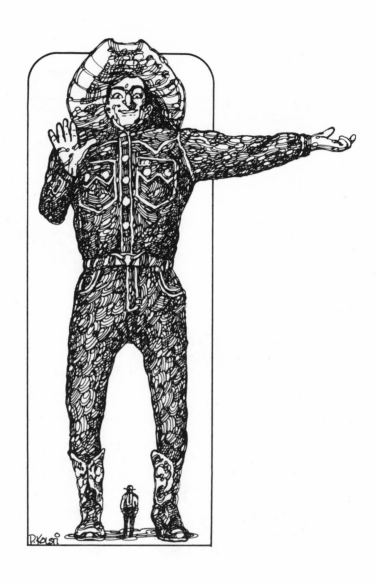

Big Tex

Big Tex has been a feature attraction of the State Fair of Texas at Dallas since 1952. He stands 52 feet high, one thumb hooked in a cocky stance, with cowboy shirt and blue jeans especially made for him every few years. His cowboy boots don't wear out — he's never had to take a step in them.

Big Tex began life as Santa Claus at Kerens, Texas, a small town about 60 miles south of Dallas in Navarro County. When moved to Dallas his face had to be redesigned. Fair officials didn't think a Texas cowboy ought to have pink cheeks — and the Kerens' Santa had what was perceived to be a lascivious wink. His first year at the State Fair Big Tex wore a sombrero, but that was replaced the next year by his 10-gallon hat. He started talking — drawling, that is — in 1953. For years his voice was taped or performed live by Old Jim Lowe, a popular area radio personality.

Although he hasn't taken a step, Big Tex gets around. In 1953 he accompanied the Dallas Jaycees to a national convention in Minneapolis, and in 1955 he appeared at Abilene Christian University's 50th anniversary party. He was at SMU for a gathering of Rotarians in 1958, and stood outside Holiday Inn Central for a broadcaster's convention in 1962.

Big Tex co-starred with Ann-Margaret and Pat Boone in the movie *State Fair,* and in 1979, rush hour motorists along Stemmons Expressway were surprised to see him in front of the Apparel Mart. He was there for a reception honoring longtime State Fair president, the late Bob Cullum. In 1983 he stood outside the Dallas Convention Center for a few days. Although 66 years younger than the State Fair, Big Tex is that exposition's best known participant.

First Street Railway in Dallas

In July 1872 when the first railroad arrived in Dallas — rather, arrived a mile to the east of Dallas — the village was still clustered around the courthouse square. Public transportation was provided by W.P. Siler's omnibuses, operating from Main and Austin, with stables at the southwest corner of Polk (Young) and Houston. But omnibuses, in Dallas' case, were hacks, seating four to six persons who were victims of mud, rain, and cold. Obviously a street railway was needed, and by October 1872, work on a line to the depot had begun.

The Dallas City Railroad Company rails ran from the Crutchfield House at Houston Street, out Main to the Houston & Texas Central depot, just east of Pacific and Central Expressway today. The one-mile line was engineered by George M. Swink, who had come to Dallas in 1868 and managed the installation (also in 1872) of Sarah Cockrell's iron toll bridge over the Trinity River. Dallas City Railroad Co. officials included T.C. Jordan, W.W. Peak, J.W. Smith, J.J. Good, W.L. Murphy, J.K.P. Record, J.W. Lane, J.W. Swindells, and Swink; an impressive civic roster.

The first Dallas street railway was laid with wooden rails topped with iron straps. Operation began February 7, 1873, carrying city and county officials and the press from the Crutchfield House to the depot and back in nine minutes, if reports are correct. Two 10-foot cars were used, one named "John Neely Bryan" in honor of the town's founder, the other "Belle Swink" after Capt. Swink's oldest daughter, a famous Dallas beauty. On that first run, Capt. Swink used Sam, his big carriage horse, because the small mules purchased for the task weren't capable of pulling the heavily loaded cars up the steep hill at Main and Ervay. When too much rain fell, boards had to be placed between the tracks to provide footing for the animals. But the streetcar line was very popular. It was the first evidence that Dallas was becoming a real city. Within a few years three other mule powered streetcar lines were serving all parts of town.

Fort Worth A Century Ago

A century or so ago, Fort Worth claimed a population of 17,000 and called itself, "Queen City of the Prairies." It was reached by three railroads from four directions, but still had lots of stagecoaches running: twice a week to Springtown, Tannahill, O'Bar, and Veal's Station and three times a week to Birdville, Grapevine, Smithfield, Bransford and Bedford. Mrs. Belle Burchill was Fort Worth's postmaster.

Proud to be known as "The City of Wells", Fort Worth had more than 100 artesian wells within its limits. But it also had a private waterworks, with Morgan Jones, president. A business directory noted, "The Holly system of waterworks, with the aid of an efficient and well equipped fire department, preclude the possibility of any serious conflagration . . ."

By the mid-1880s there were four newspapers in Fort Worth — the morning *Daily Gazette,* the afternoon *Daily Democrat,* and the *Texas Live Stock Journal* and the *Wool Grower,* both weeklies. The city had installed the Erie Telephone system, had a network of mule-powered streetcars, and had an opera house, managed by Max Elser, which seated 1,300. The streets were lighted by the Fort Worth Gas Light Company, with J.P. Smith, president, K.M. Van Zandt, vice-president, and Thomas Tidball, secretary. The gas plant was located at Weatherford and Rusk streets (now Commerce).

Architect M.R. Sanguinet, who would later design Dallas' Carnegie Library and the Wilson Building, among many famous structures, was just getting started in Fort Worth. R.L. Turner listed himself as "funeral furnisher, director and embalmer" but also as "The Enterprising Livery Man of Texas." Both funeral parlor and livery stables were at Houston and Seventh streets. And believe it or not — John Doe was a Fort Worth surgeon at the time.

Frank Buck

Frank Buck, the animal collector of "Bring 'em back alive" fame, grew up in Dallas and as a boy, got his first experience as a trapper and collector working along Turtle Creek, near his home on Welborn Street in Oak Lawn, and Five Mile Creek in Oak Cliff. Even as a boy he collected and maintained a sizable menagerie of Texas birds and animals.

He was born March 17, 1884 at Gainesville and at a young age moved to Dallas where he attended public school. At age 18 Frank Buck took a job handling a trainload of cattle being shipped to Chicago where he became a hotel bellboy. In 1904 he married a popular Chicago actress and became associated with the theater as well as becoming a newspaper correspondent.

In 1911, at age 26, he was able to indulge himself in a trip to South America where he bought several native birds, which he sold at considerable profit in New York. He was soon going into Malaya, Borneo, India, Africa and New Guinea after zoo animals. He collected several of the first animals in Dallas' zoo, in some instances donating them to his home town. In 1930 his first book (with E. Anthony) was *Bring 'Em Back Alive,* an international success as book and movie, the title of which became virtually his middle name.

At the 1933 Chicago Century of Progress Exposition he created *Jungleland,* an early theme park. He began producing movies and co-authored several other best selling books including, *Wild Cargo, Fang and Claw* (both of which were made into successful films), and his 1941 autobiography, *All In a Lifetime.* For years he had a network radio show and a touring circus. He was a popular lecturer and magazine contributor.

From his beginning as a professional, Frank Buck was known as a careful and considerate collector. In the 1980s a television series was based on his career and adventures. Frank Buck died in Houston in 1950.

The City of Preston Hollow

The North Dallas subdivision of Preston Hollow, created through developer Ira P. Deloache, was incorporated as a tax-free city in November 1939. Deloache's office, a white frame building at the northwest corner of Preston Road and Northwest Highway, became the City Hall. Joe Lawther was elected first mayor and W.H. Clark (brother of Supreme Court Justice Tom Clark) first city attorney. Officials served without pay. Lawther soon declared the municipality couldn't continue without taxes, but the council instead asked each homeowner to contribute $25 per year toward city expenses. Lawther resigned and Mart Reeves became the second mayor.

Preston Hollow government through the years included such names as Deloache, C. Dennard, A.H. Locke, and Alex Weisberg. A few months after incorporating, residents voted dry, 97-40, in a local option election. But someone found a 30-foot strip of no-man's-land between the municipalities and erected a liquor store which sold the only legal liquor from there to Missouri.

Preston Hollow town limits extended from Northwest Highway to Park Lane, and from Preston Road to Meadowbrook Drive, but a larger area went by the name. The community of Sunnybrook adjoined to the west and southwest. In the mid-30s, two large dairies, including the O'Connor Dairy, had been located on the southern corners of Preston Road and Northwest Highway. Then the west side was developed as Antony Plaza, while the east side became Varsity Village, partially owned by Southern Methodist University.

The Cotton Belt Railroad — now the route of the North Dallas Tollway — divided Preston Hollow. Meader Road Station was used by Preston Hollow commuters. Dr. Rushing's adjacent estate, between Park Lane and Walnut Hill along Inwood Road, had its own steam railroad, and what is now Ravine Drive was originally called Lone Post Road. Preston Hollow merged with Dallas in 1945.

Baseball in Dallas and Fort Worth

Full time professional baseball came to Dallas and Fort Worth in April 1888 when the Texas League of Baseball Clubs opened its first season. The Dallas team was called "Hams" and the Fort Worth team "Panthers." Fortunately, Hams wasn't retained very long by Dallas. The team eventually became the Eagles. Fort Worth's baseball teams continued to be called Panthers, or some feline derivative, for 80 more years.

Dallas played its games at Oak Cliff Park across the Trinity River from downtown. Charles H. Levis, of St. Louis, was captain and player-manager at first base. The Hams' uniforms were maroon and white. The league opened with four other cities: Austin, Galveston, Houston, and San Antonio, and was "protected" by the National League. General Admission was 25¢, 15¢ for children. A player salary limit of $1,000 per season was voted. An official "Texas League" ball, made by the Reach Company, was adopted. Umpires were paid $75 per month and railroad fare.

Leon H. Vendig was the first Dallas club president, E.R. Parry was vice president and A. Hyman, secretary. The club was capitalized at $6,000 by the board of directors: R.H. Purdy, Louis Mohrhardt, William Shea, Ollie Mansfield and C.P. Fegan. In Fort Worth, W.H. Ward was president, J.C. Berney, secretary, and A.B. Smith, treasurer.

All the clubs, with the possible exception of Dallas, lost money during the first year. Dallas won so many consecutive games that some of the clubs (including Fort Worth and Austin) dropped out and in June the league had to reorganize, with New Orleans becoming a member. When the last game was played in September 1888, Dallas led the standings with .826 and New Orleans was a far second at .619. Houston was on the bottom with .200. Despite losing money (and being reorganzied) nearly every season, the league kept playing until the Spanish-American War put a halt to it in 1898. Play resumed after two years and by 1907 the Texas League had become one of baseball's most important minor circuits.

P. KOLSTI

Colonel Belo

Colonel Alfred Horatio Belo came to Texas on horseback following the Civil War. His military title — in contrast to some of that day — was genuine. He was promoted to colonel by General Robert E. Lee after Gettysburg. He fled to Texas after Appomattox in April 1865, and that fall became business manager of the Galveston *News*.

Born in North Carolina, he grew up in the devout Moravian community of Salem. In 1866, at age 27, Belo acquired a partnership with Willard Richardson in the *News* and on Richardson's death in 1875 became principal owner and publisher of the most important newspaper in Texas. In 1881 A.H. Belo & Co. became a stock company.

Belo was a modernist in the best sense of the word. In 1876, at the Philadelphia Centennial Exposition, he watched Alexander Graham Bell demonstrate the new telephone and immediately put his name on the list to get one. By March 1878 the first Bell telephone in Texas had been installed between Belo's home and his office. In 1883 he had famed Galveston architect Nicholas J. Clayton design what was said to be the first building ever designed especially for the publishing and printing of a newspaper.

But Belo sensed that Galveston was not destined to remain the biggest city in Texas. In the early '80s he sent his young English protege, George Bannerman Dealey, to locate a promising town for a new daily newspaper and Dealey chose Dallas — for its railroads and its cosmopolitanism. Thanks to Col. Belo's continuing advocacy of "the latest machines and methods," the News began publishing in 1885 in the most modern plant, with the most advanced equipment, of any newspaper in America. The Dallas *News* had soon outstripped its sister *News* in Galveston.

Colonel Belo moved to Dallas in 1885, erecting an elegant home on Ross in 1890 which still stands — the Belo Mansion. He died April 19, 1901 while visiting in Ashville, N.C. and was buried in Salem.

Irving's Many Towns

The modern city of Irving includes more former towns than almost any municipality in the Metroplex. The pioneer village of Estelle straddled the Dallas-Tarrant County line, in northwest Irving, and Sowers (originally Buck and Breck), was at the southwest corner of today's Airport Freeway-Belt Line-Irving Boulevard interchange at Pioneer Lane, which was formerly the Birdville Road, leading to the old Tarrant County seat of Birdville. Finley Post Office, in North Irving, was near O'Connor Road and Adah Lane, and Union Bower was about where Union Bower Road today crosses Walton Walker Boulevard. The communities of Twin Wells and of Dyke City (named for the Dyccus, or Dycus, family) were reported also to have been within today's Irving boundaries.

The trail used by California-bound Forty-niners crossed the Elm Fork of the Trinity at present-day California Crossing Park and continued west to pass across Las Colinas and North Irving. But despite this early road, the Trinity lowlands held back settlement from the east for some time. Las Colinas, the city within a city built mostly on land which was formerly Ben Carpenter's Hackberry Ranch, is part of Irving.

In the 1870s the settlement of Gorbett had sprung up on Delaware Creek, but a few years later, Gorbett was moved and renamed Kit (another family name) located south of modern Irving Blvd. and the Oak Grove cemetery. The town of Lone Star, mainly a large general merchandise store, was located at the other end of Kit-Lone Star Road, a major thoroughfare until the 1960s.

Irving itself was developed by J.O. Schulze and Otis Brown in 1902 when the Rock Island Railroad built from Fort Worth to Dallas. Brown reportedly named the town out of admiration for Washington Irving, but this is not documented. Irving gradually absorbed the other communities, so that today only a few streets retain their names.

P. Kasti

Turtle Creek

Turtle Creek, the most notable waterway in Dallas, has retained a bit of its wildness while flowing through some of the most cultivated and expensive real estate in Texas. The name of the creek came from the softshell turtles seen at its mouth, which would today be about where the Dallas Tollway branches off toward I-35E. One source says the name was applied in 1837 when a handful of Texans from LaGrange, fleeing the Indians, crept across the Trinity at the mouth of Turtle Creek and noted the presence of the amphibians. However, James J. Beeman offered another, later version. His family left Bird's Fort in Tarrant County on April 1, 1842 in the region's only wagon, to settle near their friend John Neely Bryan, who was already trying to start a city that would soon be called Dallas.

"Coming down," James Beeman wrote in his memoirs, "we nooned at what we called 'Turtle Creek.' We gave it the name for having seen and caught a large softshelled turtle there — which name the creek still bears to this day."

Turtle Creek is fed by springs and even before various storm drains fed into it, it never ran dry. It heads today in Caruth Park, in University Park, between Hillcrest and Caruth streets. Two famous springs from pioneer days have been lost: Brandenburg Spring, near the Dallas Theater Center, was named for the Brandenburg family which had a farm house (actually a log cabin) nearby, and Raccoon Spring, just east of where Reverchon Park is today. The pioneers used to "jack-light" deer (hunt at night with a bright lantern) at Raccoon Spring. Calvin Cole's two-story log house at Gillespie and Cedar Springs Road had a flourishing spring nearby and a century later, when a parking garage was being built on the spot, that spring flowed so strongly it had to be shunted into a sewer because it could not be capped. It flows thus today, emptying into Turtle Creek. Turtles which gave the creek its name may often be observed sunning themselves along the top of the dam that crosses Turtle Creek at Hall Street.

Bonnie and Clyde

The film, *Bonnie and Clyde,* with Warren Beatty and Faye Dunaway, took a sympathetic view of Clyde Chesnut Barrow and Bonnie Parker Thornton — but the Depression-era Dallas outlaws were anything but heroic to law officers of North Texas and surrounding states. With their gang, Clyde and his brother caused the deaths of 10 peace officers and two citizens during a robbery and murder rampage which lasted from 1932 until 1934. A dozen or more small town banks around Dallas and Fort Worth were robbed, or believed they were robbed, by Bonnie and Clyde. The myth is so strong that visitors are assured Bonnie and Clyde held up the bank in virtually every North Texas town.

Bonnie Parker, who met Clyde Barrow because her convict husband Roy Thornton served time with him in Huntsville, was her own press agent. She wrote Dallas newspaper editors, sending bits of verse and "news" while she and Barrow were on the run. Barrow once enclosed a tongue-in-cheek endorsement of the newly-introduced Ford V-8 automobile, saying he would steal no other kind. A famous snapshot of Bonnie Parker showing her with a cigar in her mouth, is believed to have been "doctored" by a newspaper editor. She did not smoke and neither she nor Barrow drank alcohol. Despite the fact that the Barrow gang operated in four or five states, West Dallas was home base, where friends and family sheltered them.

Bonnie and Clyde were slain from ambush by Texas lawmen in Louisiana May 23, 1934. Their Dallas funerals attracted thousands. An airplane dropped flowers. When they died, Bonnie Parker was only 23 years of age and Clyde Barrow 25. The last verse of a poem Bonnie sent to a Dallas newspaper has become part of their legend.

> *Someday they'll go down together,*
> *they'll bury them side by side;*
> *To some it will bring grief, to others relief:*
> *But it's death to Bonnie and Clyde.*

Bonnie and Clyde are, in fact, buried in different Dallas cemeteries, many miles apart.

Lancaster

The town of Lancaster, in south Dallas County, was laid out in 1852 by A Bledsoe (no period, his name is simply, "A") on 40 acres he had bought from Roderick A. Rawlins, who soon became his son-in-law. Bledsoe named his new town for his birthplace, Lancaster, Kentucky. Because of its rivalry with the older, nearby village of Pleasant Run, Bledsoe was so anxious to attract settlers that it is said he gave away half his town lots.

During the Civil War, Lancaster was the site of a Confederate arms factory and munitions plant managed by Paul Henry, Sr., formerly of the French La Reunion colony and a skilled engraver. Although Tucker & Sherrard and Clark & Sherrard pistols were supposedly assembled there, and today are highly prized by collectors and among the rarest of Texas arms, few if any, are believed actually to have been produced at Lancaster during the war. Pat Garrett, who later became famous as the slayer of Billy the Kid in New Mexico, worked as a cowboy around Lancaster.

For years Lancaster was the largest town in Dallas County outside Dallas. From its beginning it was a major agriculture center and among Dallas Historical Society holdings is an 1857 patent issued to a Lancaster man for an enormous plow designed to break the packed prairie sod. In 1884 Lancaster was such a cotton shipping point it had six gins. When the town opened its first public high school, it passed a law forbidding a bar within three miles of the school — this, in effect, made Lancaster dry long before Prohibition. In 1899 Randolph Clark, one of the founders of Add-Ran College (which became Texas Christian University), opened Randolph College in Lancaster but it closed three years later. At one time Lancaster had its own railroad, The Lancaster Tap to Hutchins, and from 1912 until 1948 Lancaster was a major station on the Texas Electric interurban Railway between Dallas and Waco.

Gradually, Dallas crept south to touch Lancaster, but today the smaller town contains some of the finest 19th century restored homes and buildings in Dallas County.

Dallas Was Almost Warwick

Dallas almost *wasn't* Dallas in the first place; it was almost a town called Warwick. In 1839, two years before John Neely Bryan arrived at the Trinity River to start his town of Dallas, Warren Angus Ferris, the official surveyor of Nacogdoches County, undertook to lay out the town of *Warwick* at the Three Forks on the western edge of Nacogdoches County — which at that time stretched from East Texas to the Trinity River. Warwick would have been almost exactly where downtown Dallas is now.

On Sept. 4, 1839 Warren executed a $5,000 bond to William P. King, the conditions of which were: "Warren A. Ferris, having agreed to survey and define the limits external and internal of the City of Warwick agreeable to a plat furnished by said Ferris to said King . . ."

Ferris wrote a brother, "I have just made arrangements to survey ninety leagues for the Southern Land Co. They furnish twenty-five men, and provisions, for which I receive the sum of $5,000 good money. Isn't that splendid?" And he added, "I also hold the company's certificate for one-twelfth of the City of Warwick . . ."

But drought, sickness, and desertions stalled Ferris' first two expeditions before the Three Forks country was reached. Finally, on June 3, 1840, Ferris and King left Nacogdoches with 29 men, among them John H. Reagan, Nicholas Darnell, and Robert A. Terrell, all destined to play important roles in Texas history. But the extremely dry season had so altered the physical aspects of the area the surveyors couldn't even find the Three Forks and were unable to determine where Warwick should be. Thus, a Texas drought decided against Dallas being "Warwick." Ferris lamented, "I started with 29 men, and in six weeks I was left with but two."

But drought or not, Ferris liked the area so well that in 1846 he moved to the Three Forks and spent the rest of his life on a farm which covered Dallas' Forest Hills section, overlooking White Rock Lake.

P. KOLSTO

First Bridge Over The Trinity

In 1855, after 14 years of off-and-on ferry service, Dallas opened the first bridge over the Trinity River. Built by Alexander Cockrell, the bridge was constructed of cedar logs, cut south of town, and was 525 feet in length, which made it the longest bridge in Texas. It was considered quite an engineering feat at a time when there were few Texas bridges of any kind longer than a single span.

Cockrell's log bridge was at the foot of Commerce Street. That's where the Trinity River ran in those days. It was a covered bridge, and users paid tolls ranging from 2¢ each for sheep to 20¢ for wagons. Cockrell also improved the western approaches through the river bottom — laying logs closely together in what was called a corduroy road — so that the route was passable in all but the wettest weather.

Although built for the benefit of Dallas and citizens who lived "over the river" (as Cockrell had), the log bridge greatly aided Fort Worth, offering an all-weather crossing of the Trinity to westward-moving newcomers who were not so inclined to remain on the east bank, where Dallas was. The Dallas *Herald* reported that during a five month period, 10 to 15 immigrant wagons a day used the bridge going west. Legend says John Neely Bryan waited nervously at the west end of the log bridge late one night while John C. McCoy, his lawyer, brought legal papers to sign when Bryan was fleeing Dallas after having assaulted one of his fellow citizens.

Alexander Cockrell was shot and killed by the town marshal in 1858 and shortly after that, one span of his bridge collapsed in a flood and was never repaired. Some said the bridge had been poorly engineered or improperly erected, but as late as the 1940s some of Cockrell's old log abutments were still solidly in place on the west bank of the Trinity's former channel. Cockrell's widow, Sarah, was the chief investor in 1872 when the first *iron* bridge over the Trinity was erected at the same spot.

Why Pacific Avenue in Dallas

Ever wonder why there's a Pacific Avenue running through the heart of downtown Dallas . . . and the Pacific Ocean is 1,500 miles away? Well, the reason goes back to the 1870s. The village of Dallas had gotten its first Iron Horse when the Houston & Texas Central Railroad came through on the way north to the Red River. That made the town anxious to be a rail crossroads, the only true east-west, north-south crossroads in Texas at the time. The Texas & Pacific Railway, then at Longview, had announced plans to build west, but along the 32nd parallel, which would miss Dallas by 60 miles to the south.

Dallas leaders wanted to do anything possible to get T&P to come its way. Thus, the Dallas state representative slipped a trick clause in the T&P's charter which said the railroad must cross the H&TC "within one mile of Browder Springs." Browder Springs was one mile from the Dallas County courthouse. This made the rail executives furious and they threatened to miss Dallas proper by going a mile *south* of Browder Springs, which would have put the line two miles from Dallas — a considerable distance in those days. The city compromised by giving the T&P $100,000 worth of city bonds, 27 acres of land for station and yards, and right-of-way for track on Burleson Street, a downtown path that wasn't being put to much use.

The railroad agreed, and to celebrate, Dallas changed the name of Burleson Street to Pacific Avenue, honoring the Texas & Pacific Railway. Until 1923 the T&P's tracks, and its freight trains, ran right down the middle of the street, and until the Union Station was constructed in 1916, a downtown passenger station stood at the corner of Pacific and Lamar. Even today one may observe a notch cut from the south side of Pacific at this location where a loading dock stood.

Despite its corporate title, the Texas & Pacific Railway (now Missouri Pacific) got no closer to the Pacific than El Paso, Texas . . . and the Dallas avenue.

The Name of The Trinity

The Trinity River of Texas is made up of three main branches: the West Fork, rolling into Dallas from Fort Worth, the Elm Fork, which joins the West Fork between Dallas and Irving, and the East Fork, coming on stream just below Dallas County. In fact, in early Texas history — before there was a Dallas or Fort Worth or Irving — this entire northern section of Texas was known simply as "The Three Forks." So, you'd think that's where the Trinity got its name, wouldn't you — from its three main branches.

But as occurs so often in history, what seems logical happens not to be the case. The Trinity River was named in 1690 by Alonso de León, a Spanish officer who was initially sent from his native Cadereyta, Mexico to find, and capture, La Salle's French colony on the Texas Gulf coast. Finding Fort St. Louis abandoned, he burned the ruins. Alonso de León gave the stream the religious name of "Rio de La Santisima Trinidad," or, River of the Most Holy Trinity, probably because he crossed it on Trinity Sunday. Regardless of his reason, de León was over 200 river-miles downstream from the Three Forks and didn't know those three main branches even existed.

The Caddo Indians called the river *Arkikosa* in Central Texas and *Daycoa* nearer the coast. La Salle referred to it as "The River of the Canoes." Domingo Terán in 1691, tried to name the stream *Encarnacion de Verbo*.

Dallas restaurant owner Mario Leal had a direct connection with this 17th century expedition that named the Trinity River. Lt. Leal, a famous soldier, was his ancestor, and was an important officer with de León. Both the lieutenant and de León came from the vicinity of Monterey, Mexico. Many members of the Leal family still reside at Linares, in the area.

Hord's Ridge

The west side of the Trinity River, across from John Neely Bryan's village of Dallas, was originally in Robertson County and had little connection with the farther shore, which was part of Nacogdoches County.

However, the west side had begun to settle almost as early as the east side. Members of the Johan Narboe family, arriving there in 1843, were among the first Norwegian immigrants in Texas. Samuel Browning, a son-in-law of W.S. Peters and one of the original contractors of the Peters Colony (the 1840s group that controlled much North Texas land) moved "over the river" in 1844 but died almost as soon as he arrived. One of the oldest marked graves in Dallas County is in old Oak Cliff Cemetery, that of John W. Wright's little daughter Martha, who was born and died nearby in mid-1844.

William H. Hord gave the community its initial name. He and his family arrived from Tennessee in 1845, taking up a Peters Colony grant along Cedar Creek, around what is now Marsalis Park Zoo, from Clarendon to Davis and from Zang to Ewing. He built a cabin which still stands, and the surrounding area became known as Hord's Ridge. William Brown Miller brought his family to the Cedar Crest area in 1847, erecting his imposing home, Millermore, now in Dallas' Old City Park, prior to the Civil War. The Coombs (of Coombs Creek), the Merrifields, the Overtons and the Leonards were other important early "west side" land owners. Elder T.V. Griffin organized Dallas County's first Church of Christ there in 1846.

In the 1850 election for county seat, the town of Dallas beat Hord's Ridge in the runoff by only 15 votes. In 1884 Dallas architect James Flanders began Flanders Heights in the section around Edgefield and Walmsley, and although the development failed, some elegant, if dilapidated, structures remain. In 1886, thanks mainly to developer T.L. Marsalis, Hord's Ridge became Oak Cliff.

The Interurbans Ran Everywhere

When the 20th century dawned, Texas was a place of muddy roads and isolated communities, with no paved highways and even in cities, few paved streets. The best way to get somewhere was to catch a train. But railroad schedules weren't convenient for short trips, such as to and from work, or shopping. Then in 1902, Northern Texas Traction Company built an electric interurban line between Dallas and Fort Worth, passing through Oak Cliff, Cockrell Hill, Arcadia Park, Grand Prairie, Arlington and Handley en route. The interurbans were bigger, fancier trolley cars, flashing along at 50 miles an hour — an unheard-of speed in those days — operating every thirty minutes or hour.

Within a few years Dallas and Fort Worth were the center of the largest electric rail network in the South. The Denison and Sherman Railway, the first interurban railway in Texas (1900), became part of Texas Traction, which joined Dallas and Sherman in 1908 via Vickery, Richardson, Plano, Allen, McKinney, Melissa, Anna and Van Alstyne. In 1912 the Fort Worth Southern opened from there to Cleburne, via Burleson and Joshua. Southern Traction from Dallas began operating lines to Waco and Corsicana in 1913, the Waco line running through Lisbon, Lancaster, Waxahachie, Italy, Hillsboro, and West, and the Corsicana branch through Hutchins, Ferris, and Ennis. In 1916 Texas Traction and Southern Traction merged to become Texas Electric Railway. In January 1923 the Texas Interurban opened from Dallas to Terrell, via Mesquite and Forney, and on October 1, 1924 a Denton branch began operations by electrifying the existing M-K-T tracks to serve Hudnall, Love Field, Letot, Farmers Branch, Carrollton, Lewisville, and Lake Dallas. Both lines shut down in 1931.

The last Dallas-Fort Worth interurban ran Christmas Day, 1934. The Corsicana line was abandoned in 1941. Texas Electric, to Denison and Waco, ceased operating in 1948, ending Dallas' interurban age.

Love Field: Whose Name?

Dallas Love Field, for almost 40 years the city's municipal airport, and still one of the busiest airports in the nation, was not named for a Dallas resident. It was named for Lt. Moss Lee Love, a pioneer Army flier killed in an air crash in California — and no kin to Thomas B. Love, a Dallas political figure of that period. So far as we know, Lt. Love never visited Dallas.

Love Field was built in 1917 as an Army advanced air training center. That initial installation was a line of hangars and sheds along the northern side of the modern Love Field, overlooking Bachman Lake. Many of the aviation trainees of the period lived at Camp Dick, at Fair Park. After World War I, Love Field was bought by a group of Dallas businessmen and partially turned into an industrial park. One of the biggest cotton cloth mills in Texas was located at Love Field, as well as a famous pottery factory. Three ex-Army hangars and a landing strip on the north end continued to be used for civilian flights.

The advance of civilian aviation caused the City of Dallas to purchase 167 acres from the Love Field Company in 1927 and create one of the earliest municipal airports in the United States. Air mail service out of Dallas had begun the year before, and by 1928 several airlines were serving Love Field. During the 1930s and '40s the passenger terminal was relocated twice, on Lemmon Avenue, moving to its present location in the mid-50s. Love Field eventually became headquarters for several major airlines, including Southern Air Transport, that became American Airlines, and Braniff, which relocated to Love Field from Oklahoma in 1942.

When Dallas/Fort Worth Regional Airport opened in 1974, Love Field became the center for commuter airlines and private aviation, and today is as busy as ever.

Index

141

142